Vintage Beer Tap Markers
Ball Knobs, 1930s-1950s

George Baley

Schiffer Publishing Ltd
4880 Lower Valley Road, Atglen, PA 19310 USA

Dedication

This book is dedicated to my Mother, who recently passed away. Her daily phone calls of encouragement are missed. It is also dedicated to Barb, my best friend, whose continued patience, support, and confidence made this adventure possible. Also to my children, Heather and Jamie, both of whom I love and am very proud. And lastly, to all the good friends, living and deceased, who opened their homes to me, permitting this book to become a reality.

Library of Congress Control Number: 2003103150

Designed by Mark David Bowyer
Type set in Benguiat Bk BT/Humanist 521 BT

ISBN: 0-7643-1831-4
Printed in China
1 2 3 4

Published by Schiffer Publishing Ltd.
4880 Lower Valley Road
Atglen, PA 19310
Phone: (610) 593-1777; Fax: (610) 593-2002
E-mail: Info@schifferbooks.com
Please visit our web site catalog at **www.schifferbooks.com**
We are always looking for people to write books on new and related subjects. If you have an idea for a book, please contact us at the above address.

This book may be purchased from the publisher.
Include $3.95 for shipping.
Please try your bookstore first.
You may write for a free catalog.

In Europe, Schiffer books are distributed by
Bushwood Books
6 Marksbury Avenue
Kew Gardens
Surrey TW9 4JF England
Phone: 44 (0) 20 8392 8585
Fax: 44 (0) 20 8392 9876
E-mail: Bushwd@aol.com
Free postage in the UK. Europe: air mail at cost.

Contents

Preface

Vintage Beer Tap Markers is a reference guide for collectors and dealers to identify, evaluate, and characterize what commonly are called "ball knobs." It is directed toward early post-Prohibition knobs from more than 600 American and a dozen or so foreign breweries.

Acknowledgments

The compilation of a book on the subject of ball knobs was a task that could not be completed without the participation of a large number of collectors and breweriana enthusiasts. The cooperation of those who permitted their collections to be photographed and provided technical advice was critical to this project and is greatly appreciated. Listed below are most of the participants. A thanks goes out as well to anyone who I may have inadvertently missed and not included by name.

An extra special thanks goes to Donna Baker, my editor, for her continued patience and guidance in this, my second project with Schiffer Publishing. And of course to Bruce Waters, who worked his way through countless examples of photo setups in order to select the best possible way to display the knobs.

Andy Abel
George Arnold
Don Augenstein
Tom Ball
Jim Beaton
John Bitterman
Fred Bolton
Paul Brady
Marcia Butterbaugh
Bill Carlisle
Bob Christiansen
Dwayne Doel
John Ferguson
Jim Freeman
Dave Freimark
John Fritsch
Stan Galloway
Dave Gausepohl
Mike Gerth
Mike Gisburne
Adolf Grenke
Bob Hajicek
Larry Handy
John Harrison
Jay Herbein
"Bud" Hundenski
Chad Ireland
Dan Jeziorski
Jim Kaiser
Dave Kapsos
Bob Kay
Ron Kikta
Vic Kroll
Dave Launt
John Mlady
Larry Moore
Dick Ober
Ken Ostrow
Jim Peter
Phil Pospychala
Jim Reichmuth
Frank Rothdeutch
Don Roussin
Mike Scherer
Bob Schinski
Rick Schmidt
Tye Schwalbe
Ed Sipos
Pat Stanbaugh
Dick and Rick Strisofsky
John Upham
Dave Vajo
John Vetter
Dave Wendl
Dave Witman
Mark Zeppenfelt

Introduction

A collector's book on "ball style" tap markers was an idea that started more than fifteen years ago while I was completing my first book on *Back Bar Breweriana.* I had received a comprehensive list of knobs from a fellow collector, John Harrison, as an aide in dating statues for that book. Being an avid seeker of Michigan breweriana, I mentioned a few years ago to another friend, Bud Hundenski, that I had accumulated a fairly sizable collection of Michigan ball knobs. Bud indicated that he had a large collection of knobs from all over the country and "wouldn't it be great to do a book on ball knobs?" I retrieved John's list and we were on our way.

A year or so was spent canvassing the hobby for other collections and determining what level of interest existed amongst collector to permit their collections to be photographed. We learned that there are a finite number of major "generic" collectors, with in excess of about 300 knobs, but there are an extremely large number of collectors specializing in knobs from one state or region. Getting to those persons would be key to filling in the gaps missing from even the large collections. The strategy was to first photograph the largest collections from Bud, John, Duane Doel, and Dave Vajo. The word was then put out that photo sessions would be held at each of the major annual meetings of the ABA, ECBA, NABA, and BCCA. Collectors from around the country brought knobs for the sessions. In addition, several trips were made to major regional collectors like Adolph Grenke, John Fritsch, Dave Witman, Tom Ball, Dick Strisofsky, Dave Launt, and George Arnold to shoot their specialties.

Because there was a picture limit for the book of about 1500 photographs, experiments were conducted to establish the optimum number of knobs per picture. After much shooting and trials with backgrounds, lighting, etc., a gray background with up to three knobs was chosen. Since many of the collectors were regional in their interests, it was decided to separate the knobs first by states and then alphabetically within each state. Foreign knobs were to be listed separately, in alphabetical order by brand.

It was surmised from John Vetter's book on breweries (*The New Who's Who in Brew)* that upwards of 4000 brand names and/or types of beer were produced by about 700 breweries during the period of interest. Virtually every brand of beer was marketed in kegs to bars and taverns and required some tap-like delivery system, and therefore would have employed a tap marker. Only a fraction of the total breweries bottled and/or canned their beer. In fact, the beer can was just being introduced as a container for beer in the mid 1930s. Assuming each brand of beer averaged one to three (or more) distinct knob styles, it was hypothesized that upward of 8000 knobs may have existed from the period of the mid 1930s through the mid 1950s.

It was decided to shoot everything available from the ball knob era and to select candidates for the book at a later time. More than 2800 era knobs and over 2000 photographs were gathered by the time shooting ended. It became apparent there were too many candidates for the space available, so the decision was made to focus this first effort on basic "ball style" tap markers. The remaining, unused knobs will be included in a second book along with additional new "finds."

The book is divided into four chapters. Chapter One discusses some background on the history of tap markers, as well as dating, grading and pricing; while Chapter Two focuses on major manufacturers of the knobs themselves, including a brief treatment of styles, design, and repairs. Chapter Three showcases more than 2000 ball style knobs organized by state and then alphabetically by brand name within each state. Included in each knob's caption is the brewery (best guess in some cases), year(s) of use, and estimated value range. To converve space, abbreviated brewery names are included in the captions; the index contains a more complete description. For years early in a decade, the letter E was used before 40s or 50s; i.e., E40s for early 1940s or E50s for early 1950s. Similarly an L indicates later years in the decade, i.e. L30s or L40s. Finally, Chapter Four presents examples of knob styles that were not included in this book and offers a glimpse of what may be included in a future effort.

An Index at the end of the book contains a cross reference by knob number for all the U.S. brands brewed by each brewery listed. Included in the index is a date range when a brewery was generally in business, regardless of the name under which it operated. For a more comprehensive date range, interested readers should consult *American Breweries II* or the *New WHO'S WHO in Brew.*

We know that we missed some knobs from tiny breweries in business for only a few years. Also, minor design changes from both major and regional brands were not included. If this effort is well received, we plan to publish another book and include the additional styles/types of tap markers, including transition style knobs used shortly after the ball knob era. With that in mind, I am seeking your input in future endeavors, including making your collection available for a photography session. You may contact me through the publisher or at my personal email addresses: gbaley@attbi.com, gbaley@comcast.net, or ballknobs@aol.com. Your suggestions, including comments with regard to dating, breweries, and price information, are most welcome.

Chapter One

The Introduction of "Ball" Style Tap Markers

A Brief History of Prohibition

The temperance movement in America got a strong foothold in 1893 when the Anti-Saloon League was formed. The League, along with other anti-drinking groups such as the Woman's Christian Temperance Union, pushed for a national prohibition on alcoholic beverages. At the turn of the century, saloons proliferated at a ratio of one for every two hundred persons. Because of stiff competition, tavern owners often turned to other forms of generating revenue, including gambling and prostitution. This further intensified the movement towards prohibition, as a means of controlling the perceived deviate activities.

The passage of the Volstead Act in 1919 outlawed beverages containing more than one-half of one percent alcohol by volume. It went into effect one year later with only Connecticut and Rhode Island failing to ratify the 18th Amendment to the Constitution. With Prohibition came a dramatic reduction in the consumption of alcoholic beverages. In fact, by the early 1920s, the rate had been reduced by almost 70%. Persons desiring such beverages turned to illegal means of obtaining them, including home brewing and visiting small saloons known as "speakeasies" or "blind pigs."

Prior to Prohibition, the requirement to identify the brand of beer being dispensed in a tavern was at best a state or local requirement. Breweries sold their products to taverns through highly controlled channels. In fact, by the time Prohibition was initiated, most beer in keg form was sold through what were known as Tied Houses. These were tightly controlled by the breweries that would provide taverns a complete bar in exchange for exclusively handling only their brand of beer(s). This not only reduced the competition, it also left the tavern owners indebted to the breweries, since they often signed long term leases for the equipment provided. By the early 1900s, breweries directly controlled over 80% of the beer sold in taverns. With the coming of Prohibition, virtually all taverns failed except those that found other uses for their facility. Because many taverns defaulted on loans, the property they occupied was often taken over by the breweries. For that reason, many breweries became heavily involved in real estate during Prohibition through their holdings, often in key locations around each city.

Many of the politicians who gained office through the support for Prohibition in the late teens were voted out by the late 1920s, thus making repeal in 1933 a virtual reality. The election of Franklin D. Roosevelt, whose party campaigned heavily for the repeal of Prohibition, assured an end to the experiment.

Figure 1. Schott Brewing Co. statue. 11" chalk, c. 1934. Issued by brewery to thank newly elected President Roosevelt for ending Prohibition.

We should remember that the mood of the country in the late 1920s was less than optimistic, as we had just entered the beginning of the Great Depression. The elimination of Prohibition not only helped soothe the nation's depressed spirit, it also offered the opportunity for significant increases in employment at breweries, taverns, and suppliers of grain, equipment, and packaging materials.

Then, at 12:01 a.m. on April 7, 1933, Prohibition was officially repealed. Federal regulations provided a blanket set of rules governing the selling of alcoholic beverages, but many issues were left to each state to decide. For that reason, a crazy quilt of rules and regulations developed, many of which still remain in effect today in parts of the country. Federal and state laws governed exactly what breweries could and could not do with regard to providing assistance to taverns. This was intended in part to break the stranglehold that breweries formerly had on the distribution channels prior to Prohibition. It was at this time that the use of tap markers came into being as part of the Federal law changes. Prior to Prohibition, tavern delivery systems used taps or faucets to deliver beer from kegs at the bar. Engaging a handle or lever activated the taps. Typically the faucet had a knob, often shaped as a sphere or ball, as shown in Figure 2; hence, the name "ball knob" was born. However, the industry to this day officially refers to these identification devices as "tap markers," with the term "ball knob" being a nickname used by knob collectors.

Figure 2. Early post-Prohibition ball knob.

Why Tap Markers?

As noted, the end of Prohibition brought many new regulations to the brewing industry. Prohibition ended in 1933, yet little documentation has been uncovered that specifically deals with just how the tap marker fit in as a federal requirement. This may be due to the rapid sequence of events that occurred upon the repeal of Prohibition. With Roosevelt's election in November of 1932, repeal came quickly in 1933.

An early requirement for identification of the beer being dispensed was found in the Commonwealth of Pennsylvania Bulletin No. 19, issued on August 15, 1935. It read as follows:

> To All Licensees:
>
> Section 23, paragraph (j) of Act 398, known as the Beverage License Law, approved July 18, 1935, provides that:
>
> "It shall be unlawful for any retail dispenser to furnish or serve any malt or brewed beverages from any faucet, spigot or other dispensing apparatus unless the trade name or brand of the product served shall appear in full sight of the customer and in legible lettering upon such faucet, spigot or dispensing apparatus.
>
> This means that the lettering of the trade name or brand must appear upon the spigot or faucet or device attached or affixed securely thereto and at all times in full view of the customer.
>
> Licensees who at their own expense place the lettering or device upon the spigot or faucet are not limited as to the cost thereof, but when furnished by a brewer, distributor or importing distributor, the cost shall not exceed One ($1.00) Dollar.
>
> *The Board will allow until September 15, 1935 for all licensees to comply with the Section of the Act.*

Figure 3. Typical "ball" style tap marker.

Federal law prevented the aggregate value of all free accessories provided by breweries for the dispensing of beer to patrons from exceeding $5.00 per year. However, breweries could furnish additional accessories to taverns at no less than cost. The $5.00 included any and all devices (including tap markers) required to dispense beer.

In this presentation, we will focus on the "ball style" tap marker knobs introduced shortly after Prohibition. An example of one from Frankenmuth Brewing is shown in Figure 3 on page 7. The typical diameter of a ball knob's face is approximately 1-1/2" and the height varies between 2-1/2" and 3".

In selecting what ball knobs to include in this book, an "arm's length" rule of thumb was usually applied. This meant that if two knobs were held at arm's length and appeared virtually identical to the naked eye, only one was included. If a knob was available with both a metal and acetate insert, but both appeared similar at arm's length, the intent was not to photograph both.

Breweries may have used more than one body manufacturer to supply their ball knobs. Some brands of beer used knobs with standard inserts on one side and buttons or script on the reverse side. Other than in Figures 22 and 23, the back side of the knobs was not photographed separately here, in order to keep the amount of photos to a reasonable number.

Foreign brewed beers were also required to meet the regulations for tap identity. Included in Chapter Three is a selection of foreign brand "ball" knobs, most of which were fabricated by U.S. companies. Because we were at war during the early 1940s, many of the foreign ball knobs, with the exception of Canada and perhaps Mexico, were post-war entries.

Some U.S. breweries employed a "regular" knob for traditional keg systems and a special type of knob called a "Kooler-Keg" for keg systems requiring special hardware. As shown in Figure 4, the Kooler-Keg knob is easily recognized by a square hole at the base of the knob, as opposed to the traditional threaded opening. The same insert was often used for both the traditional style knob and the Kooler-Keg knob. If the Kooler-Keg Company provided the knob, "Kooler-Keg" was printed on the face. A squat style knob (865-867) was made by General Products for Kooler-Keg systems. To conserve page space, Kooler-Keg knobs are included within the knob section **only** if the insert was significantly different from any other regular knob face.

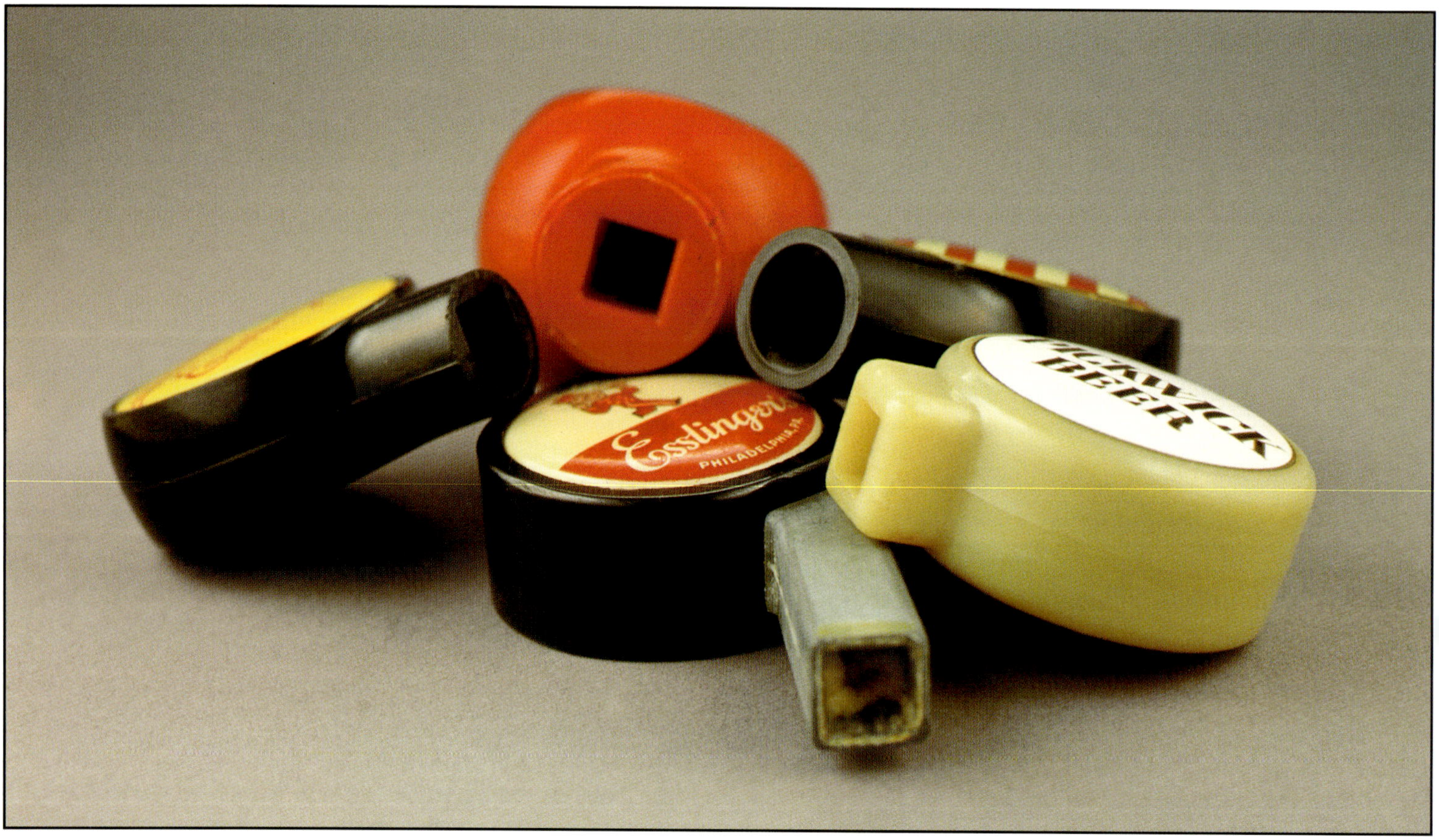

Figure 4. A pile of "Kooler-Keg" knobs.

Estimating the Age

The best source of estimating age is dated literature depicting the tap marker. Since no company sales brochures were located, we must rely mostly on knob company ads from the 1930s *Brewery Age Buyer's Guides*. These ads included actual pictures of brands of beer using the knob company's products. Experienced tap marker collectors can often identify the era of a knob by the body and insert style used. Care must be exercised, however, since an incorrect body has been often matched with an insert at some point after the original issuance. Kooler-Keg inserts sometimes are placed incorrectly in regular bodies, as shown in Figure 5 for the Bohemian Club (1326) knob. Inserts are known to have been removed from a two-insert Fisher knob (479-481) in order to make two "regular" appearing ball knobs, using bodies requiring a single insert. Inserts often turn up in the estates of persons who worked for the knob or insert companies and are often found displayed incorrectly as badges or buttons.

Figure 5. Bohemian Club with incorrect Kooler-Keg insert.

Some ball knob bodies (those made by Robbins, Fox, Fisher, and Bastian Bros., for example), and even a few inserts, included the name of the knob body manufacturer. While twenty-two knob companies are listed in Appendix B, more than a dozen "mystery" knob bodies were photographed for this book—representing companies that could not be identified, even by our experts.

Every ball knob indicates the brand of beer being dispensed and about 75% also include the brewery name and/or state where the beer was brewed. Beer can or other breweriana related books offer limited value in dating tap markers since many of the knobs represented small breweries that never marketed beer in bottles or cans. If the beer *was* bottled or canned, however, and the label contains the letters IRTP (Internal Revenue Tax Paid), we know it was made before 1950 when the legal requirement to note this on the label was stopped. Comparing the graphics, letter shape, or other symbols/logos on the knob insert to reference samples may provide more insight regarding date. During the early 1950s, for example, beers that were originally spelled with an apostrophe "s" often dropped the "s" from their spelling, as with the Kamm knobs 332 and 333 in Chapter Three.

Book and Journal Resources

The New WHO'S WHO in Brew, prepared by John Vetter (2000), is the most complete compilation of brewery brands used between the end of Prohibition, April 1933, and about 1990. This reference is especially valuable when searching for brands produced between 1933 and 1957, when the ball knob era ended. The book summarizes brand, type of beer, brewery, location, years produced, and American Brewery code for more than five thousand brand/brewery names. To search a brewery or date, one needs to know the label brand name, which is always on the knob face. Sometimes a troublesome issue is determining the actual brewery that made the beer, as many brand names were used by more than one brewery. In fact, more than fifty different breweries used Old German as a brand name for one or more of their beers! Over time, breweries came and went, were acquired by others, and the facilities moved from one city/state to another. Bob Kay, the world's expert on beer labels, has been most helpful in putting together information on dates and odd breweries.

American Breweries II, by Dale P. Van Wiersen (1995), summarizes breweries in America by the brewery name and location. It does not provide a listing of brand names, but does an excellent job of summarizing virtually every brewery in America by city and state. Often if the name of the brewery is listed on the tap marker, one can fairly accurately determine the date of the item, especially for the short-lived breweries. This book in combination with the Vetter book is a must for the breweriana collector.

The Beer Can Collector's Bible, by Jack Martells (1976), is the only beer can guidebook that provided dates for all U.S. cans described. In addition, brewery names and locations were included for both U.S. and foreign cans. Unfortunately, many of the dates are inaccurate, but at least they provide a general target from which to start. Recognize that canned beer came into being in 1935 and that ball knob type tap markers ceased to exist by the mid 1950s.

Back Bar Beer Figurines, by George Baley (2002), summarizes a wide variety of back bar statues and shelf signs, most of which came into being during the post-Prohibition period. It provides information on brands, breweries, and dates, which may be helpful in identifying ball style tap markers.

Other quality reference books may be found in the Bibliography section at the back of this book. This is by no means a complete listing of all books on the subject, but should serve as a good starting point for future work.

Four major collector groups in the U.S. publish periodic journals that contain many treatments of all aspects of the hobby. The National Association of Breweriana Advertising (NABA) is focused primarily on non-beer can related collecting of both pre-Prohibition and post-Prohibition collectibles. The primary focus of the Beer Can Collectors of America (BCCA) is beer cans, although in the past ten years a more general interest in breweriana collecting has developed. The American Breweriana Association (ABA) is heavily focused on new collectibles, with an emphasis on collector mugs and mirrors. As its name implies, The Eastern Coast Breweriana Association (ECBA) tends towards East Coast breweriana, and more closely resembles the NABA in collector interests. Each club does an excellent job of providing in-depth articles on the history of brewing and breweries. A listing of the various clubs and contact addresses is shown in Appendix A.

Pricing Tap Markers

Worth is reflected by the old phrase: "beauty is in the eyes of the beholder." Four characteristics critical to determining value are age, rarity, design, and condition. With the advent of online computer auctions like eBay, the intrinsic worth of tap markers—and ball knobs in particular—has entered a new and undefined world. Thirty years ago, the thought of a ball knob being worth more than $25 was unheard of. Today, it is not uncommon for knobs to sell for upwards of $500 or more! The higher-end knobs sell for outlandish prices when intense competition between two or three collectors occurs. Low end, common ball knobs sometimes are purported to be "rare" and are assigned excessive reserve bids.

In this book, the price range indicated for each knob is for an example in mint or near mint condition. Some knobs pictured may be "off grade." The range shown, however, is for a mint condition knob, not the one shown.

Age and Rarity

Since ball knobs were manufactured in a narrow range of less than twenty-five years (from 1933 to 1957), a wide variation in age is not a factor. Rarity is difficult to assign because of a lack of accurate records concerning production volumes. Typically, the rarest knobs are those from small breweries that survived but a few years after Prohibition; these knobs often lack the graphic detail typical of the major brand beers. It has been suggested that to be "rare," only one example can exist; however, I believe the existence of up to three appears more reasonable. Unlike other post-Prohibition era advertising, tap markers were a requirement, not a choice, of the breweries. While regulations prevented a return to the brewery-controlled taverns of the pre-Prohibition times, many small brewers still did not survive the end of the Depression years and the period through the end of World War II.

Design

For the most part, design considerations are restricted to colorful inserts and bodies. It was not until the end of ball knob era that dramatic changes in style were applied to tap marker design.

Knobs depicting colorful figures or characters are perceived to be more valuable than those without such images. Kooler-Keg style knobs are valued less than chrome or Bakelite bodied knobs.

Condition

Condition/grade does affect the value of a ball knob, as with most collectibles. Many ball knobs are in remarkably good condition. This is in part due to the fact that they were firmly affixed to the tap faucet. It was not until they were removed, tossed in drawers, or made into gearshift knobs for 1950s hot rods that they took a physical beating. In the past thirty or so years, a small number of "finds" of mint knob inserts has occurred. They usually came from the homes of persons who worked at the knob companies.

Ball style tap markers may be graded by a system using a range from 1 to 5:

Grade 1: (100% +) Insert and knob body are in pristine condition, free from chips, cracks, scratches, wear or fading.

Grade 2: (80-100%) Very minor scratches, minor wear with no chips, or cracks in insert or body.

Grade 3: (60-80%) No chips, cracks, fading, some wear. Professionally repaired knob inserts are Grade 3.

Grade 4: (40-60%) Minor chips or cracks, some slight fading and moderate wear. Non-professionally repaired knobs are generally classified as Grade 4.

Grade 5: (0-40%) Large chips, cracks, and fading, with significant wear and damage to paint and acetate face. Reserved for knobs in extremely poor condition. Best used as a "placeholder" until a better example can be secured.

Chapter Two

Manufacturing, Design, and Style

The Manufacturers

Because of the competitive requirement to gain acceptance within the brewing industry for their tap marker, most knob companies took elaborate pains to assure that taverns could easily exchange their knob (and beer) for another brand. Most tap systems used a standard 1/4" thread, making interchangeability easy. With the exception of the Kooler-Keg system, virtually all knobs were fairly interchangeable with the use of an appropriate adapter. Ironically, a couple of knob manufacturers touted their knobs as being "substitution proof," a fact that is somewhat contrary to the interchangeability concept they also promoted. Four companies (American Emblem, Bastian Bros., Fisher, and Robbins) manufactured more than 80% of the "ball style" tap markers.

Figure 7. Neuweiler paperweight from American Emblem. Rare. c. 1936.

American Emblem

Maker of Bakelite, plastic, and metal bodies, the American Emblem (AE) Company knob inserts always employed colorful, hard-fired enamel on a metal substrate. The AE insert employed an 8-pointed star as a gripping feature. More brands of beer used American Emblem knobs than any other. Figure 6 shows an advertisement from the *Brewery Age 1936 Buyer's Guide*. The later version of AE plastic knobs are characterized by their taller height and double line along the side. A rare go-with desk paperweight featuring a Neuweiler Beer knob from AE is shown in Figure 7.

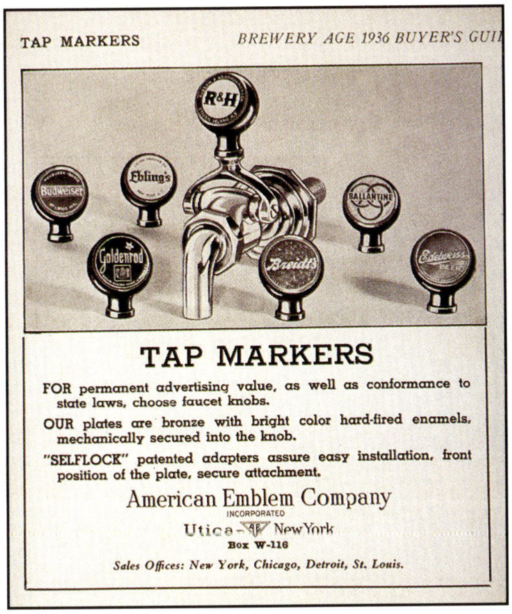

Figure 6. American Emblem ad, c. 1936.

Examples of American Emblem knobs shown in Chapter Three: Knob 913 (Bakelite); Knob 749 (plastic); Knob 1070 (metal).

Bastian Bros.

Another traditional knob company, Bastian Bros. produced knobs employing Bakelite (pre-war) or plastic (post-war) bodies and celluloid/acetate inserts. The pre-war knobs used inserts that were held on with six prong clips while the post-war knobs used inserts held on by friction or adhesive. The inserts were referred to as Lustra-Metal or Chromoloid and consisted of celluloid/acetate disks over a paper disk.

Figure 8 shows an example from a mid 1930s ad for Bastian Bros. knobs. Very rarely were painted or porcelain metal inserts used by Bastian Bros. The company name "Bastian Bros." is found embossed in the side of the knob. By the early 1950s, Bastian Bros. was also making the "Tin Can" style knob as shown in Chapter Four.

Figure 8. Bastian Bros. ad, c. 1936.

Examples of Bastian Bros. knobs shown in Chapter Three: Knob 779 (pre-war; six prong insert); Knob 937 (post-war; friction insert).

Fisher Products

Fisher knobs are characterized by their slightly taller profile. Over the years, they made at least three design changes, going from Bakelite, to Plaskon (plastic), and finishing with a two insert plastic version shown on the right in Figure 9. Fisher knobs almost always use a three prong metal insert that is enamel painted. Fisher knobs are usually embossed "True Name Patented" on one side and "Fisher Products Inc., Syracuse, N.Y." on the other. A Fisher ad from the 1930s is shown in Figure 10.

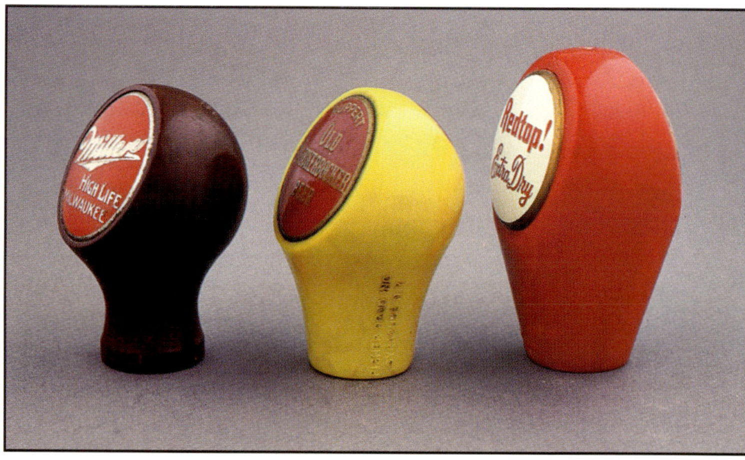

Figure 9. Three Fisher style knobs.

Figure 10. Fisher ad, c. 1936.

Examples of Fisher knobs shown in Chapter Three: Knob 1945 (early Fisher, c. late 1930s); Knob 900 (mid Fisher, c. 1940s); Knob 1115 (later two-sided Fisher, c. early 1950s).

Robbins

Robbins' round chrome shape depicts durability, as characterized by the early metal knobs. They are only found with porcelain or screened enamel metal inserts. As time and competition increased, Robbins converted to plastic bodies, but always maintained their metal inserts. A classic 1948 Robbins ad is shown in Figure 11 and a go-with advertising foam scraper is shown in Figure 12.

Figure 11. Robbins ad, c. 1948.

Figure 12. Robbins foam scraper, c. late 1930s. Rare.

Robbins chrome knobs always have their name debossed on the rear lower portion of the neck. A very similar style to Robbins are knobs from Fox Manufacturing, of Cincinnati, Ohio. It is unclear if Fox was a sub-contractor, division of, or competitor to Robbins. Figure 13 shows a comparison of knobs from Fox (left) and Robbins (right). In the late 1940s, Robbins felt the pressure to provide for knobs with a larger face area and reduced cost. Thus, they introduced a taller and flatter plastic knob, several examples of which are shown in Figure 14.

Figure 13. Comparison of Fox and Robbins knobs.

Figure 14. A bevy of Robbins knobs.

Examples of Robbins knobs shown in Chapter Three: Knob 1302 (standard chrome); Knob 1707 (late 1940s plastic).

Fox

The round chrome shape of Fox knobs makes them similar to the Robbins metal knobs. Like those from Robbins, they are only found with porcelain or screened enamel metal inserts.

Example of Fox knob shown in Chapter Three: Knob 1629 (standard chrome).

Green Duck

Employing a classic black Bakelite body, Green Duck of Chicago always used a metal-based insert with enamel. The insert has a flat metal tab soldered to the back of the insert. The insert is removed by inserting a screwdriver into the bottom-threaded hole and removing the screw. The nearly round shape characterizing the classic profile of the Green Duck design and the "neck ring" at the bottom of the knob are shown in Figure 15, in an ad from the mid 1930s. Green Duck knobs are embossed with the name "Green Duck" on the stem and are easily identified by the neck ring directly below the large ball. A rare knob go-with, a button advertising Green Duck, is shown in Figure 16. Based on actual invoices, it has been reported that the cost of Green Duck knobs was a hefty $0.40 to $0.50 each to the breweries! Wouldn't you like a dozen at that price?

Figure 16. Green Duck button ad, c. 1940s. Rare.

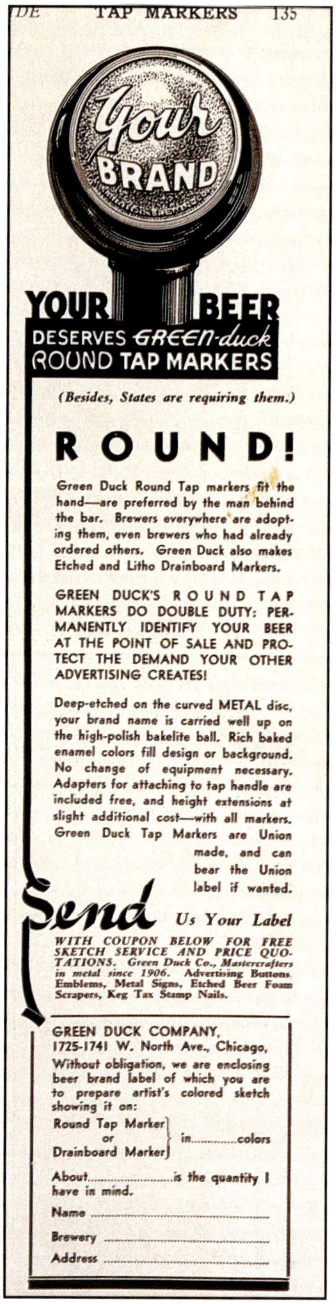

Figure 15. Green Duck ad, c. 1936.

Examples of Green Duck knobs shown in Chapter Three: Knobs 194 and 204.

Krest Manufacturing

Krest knobs were somewhat unique in that they were made from a material called Catalin. Ball style knobs from Krest have been reported in only three colors—green, red, and yellow—although the manufacturer claimed unlimited colors were available. The insert in a Krest knob is a larger diameter than most other knob inserts. A Krest ad from the 1930s (Figure 17) shows an example of the Krest style knob. Since Catalin was a material commonly used in the manufacture of radio bodies/cases of the 1930s, it is likely that other knob colors may surface. Krest inserts contained only porcelain or enamel inlay disks, never acetate/celluloid.

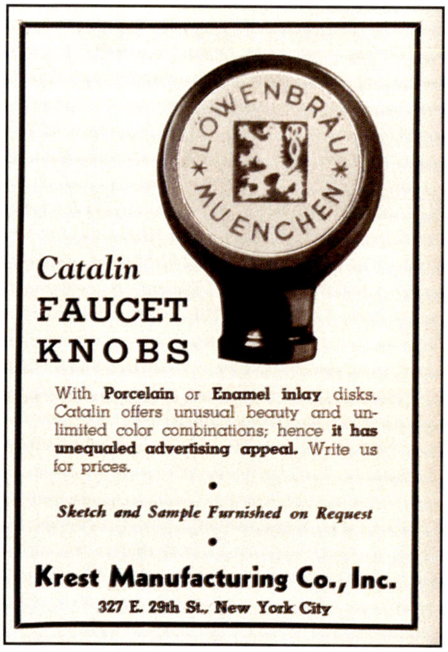

Figure 17. Krest ad, c. 1936.

Examples of Krest knobs shown in Chapter Three: Knob 857 (shorter); Knob 859 (taller); Knob 1117.

New Art Specialties

New Art was a manufacturer of traditional Bakelite bodies. They generally used a flat, stamped, or enamel fired metal insert. The inserts on their knobs were cast into the Bakelite body. The company name is marked on the neck or base. An ad from the 1930s for New Art Specialties is shown in Figure 18.

Figure 18. New Arts Specialties ad, c. 1936.

Examples of New Art Specialties knobs shown in Chapter Three: Knob 202; Knob 1220.

Selimore

Selimore made primarily Bakelite knobs for a wide variety of breweries. The bodies are not marked and are difficult to identify with any particular brand. They also made the plastic torpedo style knob with the round shaped back and an acetate insert, as shown in Figure 19,

Figure 19. A smattering of Selimore knobs.

Example of Selimore knob shown in Chapter Three: Knob 1616 (round back torpedo).

General Products

General Products made the torpedo style knobs with a more pointed, cone-like shaped back and metal enamel inserts, as shown in Figure 20. They were also responsible for producing knobs with square holes that could be used on a Kooler-Keg system using traditional inserts. These knobs were not identified by the Kooler-Keg logo, and consistently used an acetate insert for Kooler-Keg replacement knobs.

Figure 20. A group of General Products knobs.

Example of General Products knob shown in Chapter Three: Knob 58 (cone back torpedo).

Clark C. Merritt

One of the "mystery" knob companies is Clark C. Merritt, of Long Branch, New Jersey. Figure 21 shows a paperweight that appears to contain the same torpedo style knob used by Selimore, as shown in Figure 19 above. Since the knobs are not marked, one may speculate a relationship between the two companies. Some difference appears in the angle of the taper of the metal stem attached to the plastic body.

Figure 21. Merritt paperweight, c. unknown. Rare.

Design Considerations

Themes

With the exception of some of the character knobs (an example of which is shown in Chapter Four), little opportunity existed for creativity in ball knob design. Breweries typically used advertising themes for years and employed complementary graphics on the knob where physically possible. Examples of such themes are the Drewry's Mountie, Frankenmuth's dog, Rolling Rock's horse, and Old Reading's Gus.

Buttons and Script

Tap markers were intended to provide assurance to the customer that the proper brand of beer was being dispensed. However, the primary face of the knob containing the brand info was seen only by the bartender unless the knob face was turned towards or faced the customer! Some ball knobs did provide beer brand identification on both the front and back, as shown in Figures 22 and 23. Some manufacturers also included a short worded message or tiny button on the rear side of the knob that faced the customer and/bartender.

Figure 22. Front and rear of button style Krueger knob.

Figure 23. Front and rear script style Old Style knob.

Angle Cuts

Several knob companies employed various "angle-cut" style knobs, which also addressed the issue of allowing the customer to know the brand of beer being dispensed. This style was used on late 1940s and early 1950s knobs. They were part of the transition period from ball style knobs to what has become known today as tap handles. Figure 24 shows a side view of three different forms of "angle cuts."

Figure 24. Angle cut varieties.

The Manufacturing Process

The earliest insert-style knobs were made of Bakelite and employed a molding process. The Bakelite resin was poured into the mold. After curing, the knobs were removed from the mold, and the seam line was sanded and polished. Bakelite knobs were always black or brown.

After the war, injected plastic technology came into vogue. Plastic knobs are characterized by their seams and are found in a wide variety of colors.

Inserts were placed in the knob in a manner consistent with the design of the body. Some used friction, some adhesives, and others various forms of grippers or screws accessed through the threaded hole at the bottom of the knob.

Figure 26. Fisher knobs and inserts.

Insert Styles

Metal

Metal inserts made from brass or aluminum disks were the most durable type of material used in traditional ball knobs. For some brands, the blanks were stamped with a second impress and painted with an enamel or porcelain finish that required a special heat firing. Various methods of holding the insert in the knob were used. Figure 25 shows three different gripper-type inserts, Figure 26 shows the Fisher body and insert, and Figure 27 highlights Robbins style knobs. Each style of insert required a specific knob body type to function properly, and normally would not permanently fit in a competitor's body. Figure 28 shows a comparison between (clockwise, from left) an adhesive-held insert, an early Green Duck insert, an American Emblem insert, and a Fisher insert.

Figure 27. Robbins knobs and inserts.

Figure 25. Inserts for various knobs.

Figure 28. Comparison among various inserts.

Acetate

Acetate inserts were prepared using a process of printing text on clear acetate/celluloid flat stock. The inserts were then stamped out and the disks formed/wrapped around a metal disk, using a process similar to making political buttons. Figure 29 presents various acetate inserts prior to being wrapped around a disk. Sometimes a piece of paper was placed between the acetate insert and the metal disk. The insert was fastened to the knob body either by friction or through the use of an adhesive. This style insert was very susceptible to heat and water damage.

Figure 29. Acetate insert disks.

Foil Stickers

The use of foil stickers was primarily a means for breweries to allow a less expensive and rapid changeover for brands when seasonal beers like bock, dark beers, or ale did not permit or merit the generation of a regular ball knob. Breweries provided taverns with a sheet of aluminum foil stickers. The back of the foil was peeled off and the sticker placed directly onto the flat surface of the knob.

Knobs shown in this book with foil stickers are identified by an (f) after the price range. The value of such knobs is significantly less than if the knob contains a traditional insert made of metal or acetate. Dealers currently operating on computer auction sites like eBay often purport these sticker knobs to be rare, when in fact they are not. Figure 30 shows a large collection of foil stickers provided by Dick Strisofsky. Foil faced knobs are valued at around $25-50 with stickers often selling for $10-20, or just a bit more than the cost of an old knob intended for repairing a bad body. Sometimes the value of the original knob, under a foil sticker, is significantly more than the knob with the sticker. As a result, there may be a temptation to "peel off" the foil sticker in hopes of finding a true treasure. If you do so, you may be left with a very common knob or then again a really rare find. Good luck!

Figure 30. Foil stickers.

Back Buttons

A less common design feature on some knobs was a rear button or insert, as shown in Figures 22 and 23 above. The same front insert was often used on a knob with and without the back button.

Repairs, Reproductions, and Fakes

Repairs

Collectors set the majority of the value of a knob based on the condition of the insert. If a plastic or Bakelite knob body is damaged, another can often be substituted and make a displayable item. If the insert is damaged, however, any repair can be a formidable task. Damaged acetate/celluloid inserts do not lend themselves to repair. If water has gotten under the acetate face and caused damage, the value of the knob is significantly reduced. Someone familiar with restoration, however, can rejuvenate metal inserts with screened or painted enamel or porcelain.

Reproductions and Fakes

To date, no reports of reproductions or fakes have been made other than the R & H knob shown with a foam scraper holder barrel in Figure 31. It appears that the insert from a foam scraper holder barrel was converted into an insert for a Krest Manufacturing knob, which is capable of holding a larger diameter disk. Like any hobby where rarity equates to dollars, however, there may come a time when someone begins reproducing some of the rarest knobs or inserts.

Figure 31. Fake R & H knob.

Chapter Three

"Ball" Knob Style Tap Markers

By 1934, about seven hundred breweries were back in business. On July 1, 1935, thirty-eight states, plus the District of Columbia, Alaska, and Hawaii, had breweries that were qualified to operate. During the next fifteen years, the Alaska and South Dakota breweries ceased operations, North Carolina got into the business, and New Mexico had one come and go.

By July 1, 1949, there were still thirty-eight states, plus DC and Hawaii, brewing beer in about four hundred breweries. There were no breweries, during the post-Prohibition ball knob era, in the following states: Arkansas, Kansas, Maine, Mississippi, North Dakota, South Carolina, and Vermont. One brewery did operate for a very short time in Alabama, but it is unclear whether they ever had a ball knob.

This chapter is organized into United States ball knobs first by state and then alphabetically by brand name within each state, with foreign brands organized separately. Each knob has been assigned a number, starting with 1 and ending with more than 2000; where more than one knob is shown in a photograph, the numbers in the caption start with the knob on the left. Note that the knobs are arranged in column format on each page, with the numbers going up and down. Since the brand name of beer that the knob advertises is clearly seen in the photograph, it is not included in the knob's description. Instead, the name following the number (for U.S. brands) is that of the brewery that produced the beer. For foreign brands, both the brand name and country of origin are listed, but not the brewery.

The captions also include the estimated year(s) the knob was in use. (To save space, the years have been shortened to just the last two numbers, i.e., 36-38 represents 1936-1938. As noted earlier, the letters E and L indicate "early" and "late" respectively, as in E40s for early 1940s or L30s for late 1930s.) In many cases, a fairly exact year was assigned; this was based on other reference materials, the time frame when certain knobs were made, and input from collectors. For some knobs where the brand existed for only a few years, the dates from John Vetter's *The New WHO'S' WHO In Brew* were used.

An estimated price range for each knob was also established, based on input from collectors who participated in the project and to a lesser extent by computer web-based auctions. In most cases, the value range represents a consensus, but there were some debates on price—especially for the high-end knobs that generate fierce competitive bidding among a few collectors. For that reason, the highest value knobs were estimated at $250 and up. Kooler-Keg knobs are not as collectible as traditional knobs and therefore bring less. The same holds true for foil inserts, whether they are on a knob or not. And lastly, foreign ball knobs do not command a premium price in the U.S. market and generally sell for less than $50.

United States Breweries

The attrition of breweries in the U.S. from 1934 through 1950, and the practical end of the ball knob era, is reflected in statistics shown with each state section. The key dates summarize the number of breweries authorized to produce beer in 1935, 1945, and 1949 for each state where breweries existed. The Index on page 192 shows the page numbers where each state's knobs can be found.

Alaska

No examples of ball style tap knobs from Alaska were found.

1935-3
1945-0
1949-0

Arizona

1935-1
1945-1
1949-1

1. Arizona, c. 40s, $100-175.
2. Arizona, c. 38, $100-175.
3. Arizona, c. 47, $175-250.

4. Arizona, c. 36-49, $250+.

5. Arizona, c. 40s-E50s, $250+.
6. Arizona, c. 40s-E50s, $250+.

California

1935-41
1945-20
1949-19

7. Aztec, c. 35, $100-175.

8. Acme, c. 40s, $50-100.
9. Acme, c. 40s, $50-100.
10. Acme, c. 48, $50-100.

11. Acme, c. 41, $50-100.

12. Acme, c. 48, $50-100.

13. Buffalo, c. 36-39, $175-250.

14. Buffalo, c. 36-39, $175-250.
15. Buffalo, c. 36-39, $100-175.

16. San Francisco, c. L40s, $100-175.

17. Los Angeles, c. 36-37, $100-175.

18. Eastside, c. 53-57, $100-175.

19. Louis Eckert, c. 36-43, $250+.

20. Pacific, c. L30s-40s, $100-175.

21. Vernon, c. 34-43, $250+.

22. Golden West, c. 36-38, $100-175.

23. Golden West, c. 36-38, $100-175.

24. Milwaukee, c. 35-50, $175-250.

25. Grace Bros., c. L30s-40s, $175-250.

26. Grace Bros., c. L30s-E40s, $100-175.

27. Grace Bros., c. 55-57, $175-250.

28. General, c. L40s, $50-100.

29. Maier, c. E50s, $100-175.

30. Fresno, c. 36-40, $250+.

31. Kern, c. 34-40, $250+.

32. Mission, c. 40, $100-175.

33. Mission, c. 40, $50-100.

34. Rainier, c. 40s, $100-175.

35. Rainier, c. 40s, $100-175.

36. Regal Amber, c. 40s, $100-175.
37. Regal Amber, c. 40s, $175-250.

38. Rainier, c. L30s, $100-175.

39. Pacific, c. 36-43, $100-175.

Colorado

1935-5
1945-6
1949-4

40. Ph. Schneider, c. 36-39, $250+.

41. Adolph Coors, c. 36-49, $250+.
42. Adolph Coors, c. 43, $250+.

43. Adolph Coors, c. 43, $250+.

44. Ph. Schneider, c. 53-55, $250+.

45. Tivoli-Union, c. 40s, $100-175.

46. Tivoli-Union, c. 40s, $100-175.

47. Walter, c. 40s-E50s, $100-175.

48. Walter, c. 40s-E50s, $100-175.
49. Walter, c. L30s-40s, $100-175.

Connecticut

1935-12
1945-5
1949-2

50. Wehle, c. 38-43, $100-175.

51. Wehle, c. 34-40, $1-25.

52. Cremo, c. 40s-E50s, $100-175.

53. Cremo, c. 40s-E50s, $50-100.
54. Cremo, c. 40s-E50s, $50-100.
55. Cremo, c. 40s-E50s, $50-100.

56. Hull, c. 46-50, $50-100.
57. Hull, c. 46-50, $50-100.

58. Hull, c. 46-50, $50-100.
59. Hull, c. 46-50, $100-175.

60. Bridgeport, c. 36-41, $175-250.

61. Largay, c. 36-44, $100-175.

62. Wehle, c. 36-43, $50-100.

63. New England, c. L40s, $175-250.

64. Bridgeport, c. 36-38, $175-250.

65. Bridgeport, c. 36-41, $175-250.

66. Largay, c. 36-44, $100-175.
67. Largay, c. 36-44, $100-175.

68. Cremo, c. 40s, $175-250.

69. Cremo, c. 40s-E50s, $100-175.

District of Columbia

1935-2
1945-1
1949-1

72. Chr. Heurich, c. 40-48, $100-175.

Delaware

1935-1
1945-2
1949-2

73. Del Mar Va, c. 42, $100-175.

74. Diamond State, c. 40s-E50s, $100-175.

75. Diamond State, c. 40s-E50s, $50-100.

Florida

1935-11
1945-6
1949-6

76. American, c. 40-57, $100-175.

77. American, c. 40-57, $100-175.

Georgia

No knobs were photographed from the only Georgia brewery, Atlanta Co.

1935-1
1945-1
1949-1

70. Wehle, c. 36-41, $100-175.
71. Wehle, c. 40, $50-100.

Hawaii

1935-6
1945-2
1949-5

78. Hawaii, c. 36-44, $250+.

Idaho

1935-5
1945-4
1949-3

79. Sunset, c. 37-41, $250+.

80. Overland, c. L30s-E40s, $250+.

Illinois

1935-62
1945-39
1949-32

81. Atlas, c. 53, $100-175.
82. Atlas, c. 53, $175-250.
83. Atlas, c. 53, $100-175.

84. Atlas, c. L30s-E40s, $250+.

85. Manhattan, c. 38-45, $250+.

86. White Eagle, c. 35-42, $175-250.
87. White Eagle, c. 33-50, $175-250.

88. Ambrosia, c. 40s, $100-175.
89. Ambrosia, c. 40s, $175-250.

90. South Side, c. 34-37, $250+.

94. Atlantic, c. 40s-E50s, $250+.

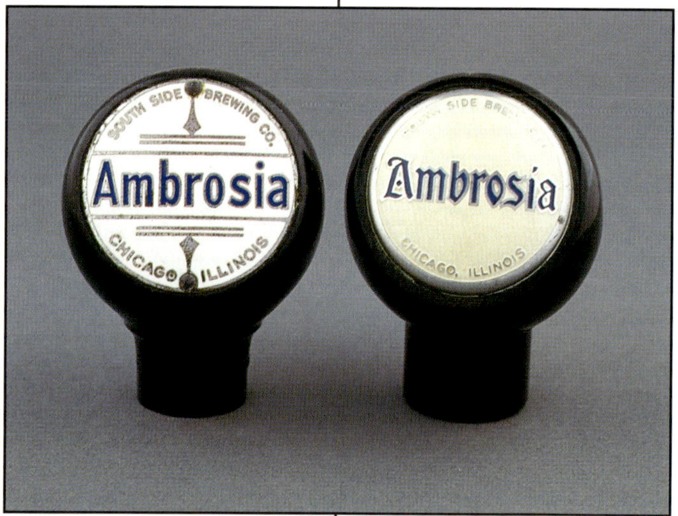

91. South Side, c. 40s, $250+.
92. South Side, c. 40s, $100-175.

95. Atlas, c. L30s-E40s, $250+.

93. Stenson, c. 36-43, $175-250.

96. Atlas, c. L30s-E40s, $175-250.
97. Atlas, c. L30s-E40s, $175-250.
98. Atlas, c. L30s-E40s, $175-250.

99. Atlas, c. L30s-E40s, $100-175.
100. Atlas, c. L30s-E40s, $50-100.
101. Atlas, c. L30s-E40s, $50-100.

102. Monarch, c. L30s-E40s, $250+.

103. Aurora, c. 36-39, $250+.

104. Huntley, c. 34-38, $175-250.

105. Prima, c. 35-38, $250+.
106. Prima, c. 35-38, $250+.

107. Best, c. L30s-E40s, $250+.

108. Best, c. 40s-E50s, $100-175.

109. Birk's, c. 35, $175-250.

110. Bismark, c. 37, $100-175.
111. Bismark, c. 38, $175-250.

112. Bluff City, c. 35, $175-250.

113. Roosevelt, c. 36-38, $250+.

114. Joliet Citizens, c. E50s, $175-250.

115. Bohemian, c. E50s, $175-250.
116. Bohemian, c. E50s, $50-100.
117. Bohemian, c. 50-52, $100-175.

118. Atlantic, c. E50s, $175-250.

119. Monarch, c. 36-38, $175-250.

120. Warsaw, c. 40s, $250+.

121. Warsaw, c. 40s, $100-175.
122. Warsaw, c. 40s, $100-175.

123. McDermott, c. 35, $175-250.

124. Manhattan, c. 44-47, $175-250.

125. Manhattan, c. 40s-E50s, $250+.

126. Manhattan, c. 40s-E50s, $175-250.
127. Canadian Ace, c. 40s-E50s, $100-175.
128. Canadian Ace, c. 40s-E50s, $100-175.

129. Canadian Ace, c. 40s-E50s, $25-50 (f).

130. Canadian Ace, c. 40s-E50s, $25-50 (f).

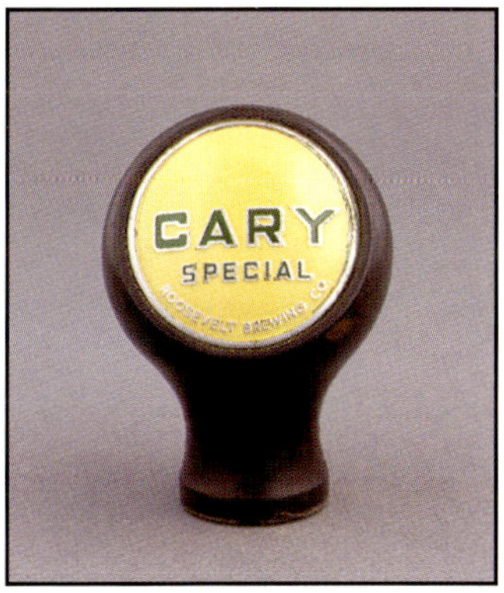

131. Roosevelt, c. 36-38, $250+.

132. White Eagle, c. 35-43, $175-250.
133. White Eagle, c. 35-43, $175-250.

134. Birk Bros., c. 36, $250+.

135. Peoria, c. 34-40, $250+.

136. Joliet Citizens, c. L40s, $250+.

137. Joliet Citizens, c. L40s, $100-175.
138. Joliet Citizens, c. L40s, $100-175.

139. Ruff-Reidel, c. L40s, $175-250.

140. Hoerber, c. 36-41, $175-250.

141. Hoerber, c. 36-41, $175-250.

142. Rock Island, c. 36-39, $250+.

143. Dick Bros., c. 39, $50-100.

144. Schoenhofen-Edelweiss, c. L30s, $50-100.
145. Schoenhofen-Edelweiss, c. L30s $100-175.
146. Schoenhofen-Edelweiss, c. L30s, $50-100.

147. Best, c. 51, $100-175.
148. Best, c. 51, $100-175.

153. Westminster, c. 36-37, $250+.

149. Monarch, c. 40s-E50s, $175-250.

150. Monarch, c. 40s-E50s, $100-175.
151. Monarch, c. 40s-E50s, $175-250.
152. Monarch, c. 40s-E50s, $100-175.

154. Garden City, c. 38-47, $250+.

155. Garden City, c. 38-47, $250+.

156. South Fork, c. 36-38, $100-175.

157. Illinois, c. 38-40, $175-250.

158. Fecker, c. 36-39, $250+.

159. Fortune Bros., c. 36-49, $175-250.
160. Fortune Bros., c. 36-49, $250+.
161. Fortune Bros., c. 36-49, $175-250.

162. Peter Fox, c. 42, $25-50 (f).
163. Peter Fox, c. 40s-E50s, $50-100.
164. Peter Fox, c. 42, $50-100.

165. Fritz, c. 36-37, $250+.

166. Gambrinus, c. 35, $250+.

167. Garden City, c. L40s, $175-250.

168. Garden City, c. 40s-E50s, $25-50 (f).

169. Gast, c. 47-49, $175-250.

170. Gipps, c. 40s-E50s, $175-250.

171. Gipps, c. 40s-E50s, $175-250.

172. Gipps, c. 40s, $175-250.

173. United States, c. 40s, $50-100.
174. United States, c. 40s, $50-100.

175. Prima, c. 36-41, $250+.

176. Prima, c. 36-41, $250+.

177. Star Union, c. 40s-E50s, $175-250.
178. Star Union, c. 40s-E50s, $175-250.

179. Best, c. 40s-E50s, $250+.
180. Best, c. 40s-E50s, $250+.

181. Schott, c. L30s-E40s, $250+.

182. Hoerber, c. 36-41, $100-175.

183. Illinois, c. 34-39, $250+.

184. Patrick Henry, c. 36-39, $250+.

185. Prima-Bismark, c. 36-41, $175-250.

186. Keeley, c. L30s-E40s, $100-175.
187. Keeley, c. L30s-E40s, $175-250.
188. Keeley, c. L30s-E40s, $100-175.

189. Keeley, c. L30s-E40s, $50-100.
190. Keeley, c. L30s-E40s, $100-175.
191. Keeley, c. L30s-E40s, $100-175.

192. Keeley, c. L30s-E40s, $250+.

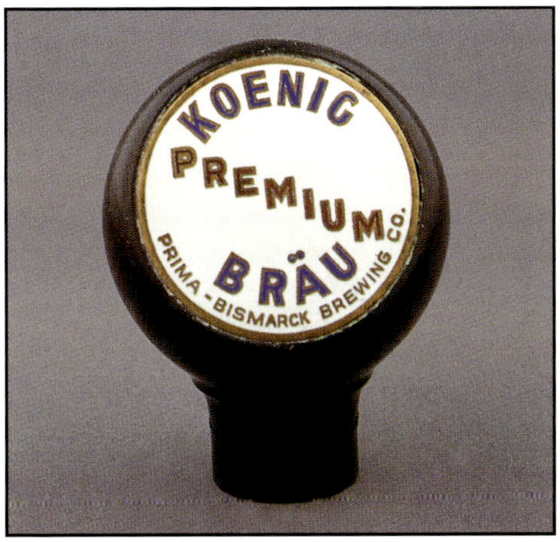

193. Prima-Bismark, c. 36-41, $250+.

194. Bismark, c. 36-41, $175-250.
195. Bismark, c. 36-41, $100-175.
196. Bismark, c. 36-41, $250+.

197. Koller, c. L30s-40s, $250+.

198. Wm. J. Lemp, c. 40, $250+.
199. Wm. J. Lemp, c. 40, $250+.

200. United States, c. 34-39, $175-250.

201. United States, c. 34-39, $175-250.

202. Malt Marrow, c. 35-38, $100-175.

203. Manhattan, c. L30s-E40s, $175-250.
204. Manhattan, c. L30s-E40s, $175-250.

205. Mound City, c. 35-43, $250+.

208. Peter Hand, c. 40s-E50s, $175-250.
209. Peter Hand, c. 40s-E50s, $175-250.
210. Peter Hand, c. 40s-E50s, $100-175.

206. McAvoy, c. 48-49, $250+.

207. McHenry, c. 34-43, $250+.

211. Peter Hand, c. 51, $50-100.

212. Monarch, c. 40, $25-50 (f).

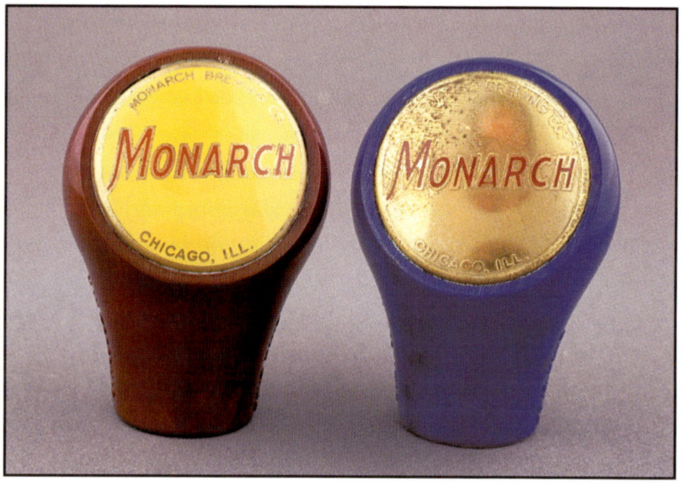

213. Monarch, c. 40, $100-175.
214. Monarch, c. 40, $100-175.

215. Monarch, c. 40s-E50s, $175-250.
216. Monarch, c. 40, $50-100.

217. Ambrosia, c. L30s-40s, $175-250.
218. Ambrosia, c. L30s-40s, $100-175.
219. Ambrosia, c. L30s-40s, $100-175.

220. Old Abbey, c. 35-41, $250+.

221. Bismark, c. 38-40, $250+.

222. Garden City, c. L30s-40s, $250+.
223. Garden City, c. L30s-40s, $175-250.

224. Garden City, c. L30s-40s, $100-175.

225. Superior, c. 36-41, $175-250.

226. Fredericks, c. 35-41, $250+.

227. Peter Fox, c. 40s-E50s, $250+.

228. Warsaw, c. E40s-L40s, $25-50.

229. Rock Island, c. 36-39, $250+.

230. Manhattan, c. 43-47, $250+.

231. Joliet Citizens, c. L40s, $175-250.

232. Westminster, c. 36-37, $250+.

233. Star Peerless, c. 40s-E50s, $250+.

234. Pilsen, c. 36, $175-250.

235. Garden City, c. L30s-40s, $250+.

236. Illinois, c. 35-41, $250+.

237. South Fork, c. 36-38, $250+.

238. Peter Hand, c. E50s, $250+.
239. Peter Hand, c. E50s, $50-100.
240. Peter Hand, c. E50s, $175-250.

248. Mound City, c. 40, $175-250.

241. Illinois, c. 35-41, $250+.

242. Pioneer, c. L30s-E40s, $250+.

243. Hoerber, c. 36-41, $175-250.

244. Prima-Bismark, c. 36-41, $175-250.
245. Prima-Bismark, c. 36-41, $175-250.

246. Garden City, c. 40s-E50s, $175-250.
247. Garden City, c. 40s-E50s, $175-250.

249. Illinois, c. 35-41, $250+.

250. Stecher, c. 36-40, $250+.

251. Galena, c. 35, $250+.

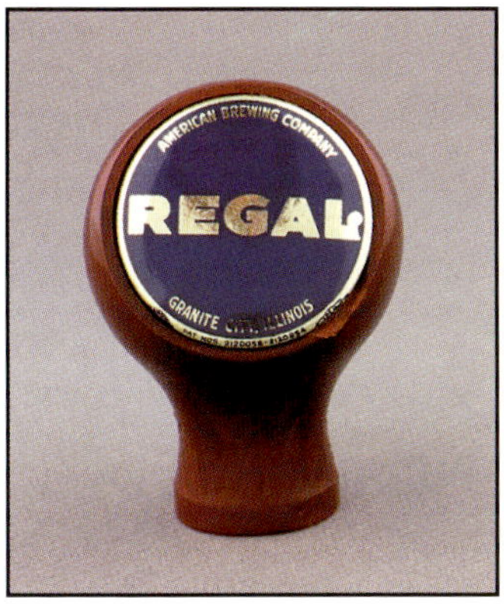

252. American, c. 38-40,
$175-250.

253. Reisch, c. 40s-E50s, $100-175.
254. Reisch, c. 40s-E50s, $175-250.

255. United States, c. 40s-E50s, $50-100.
256. United States, c. 40s-E50s, $50-100.

257. United States, c. 42, $50-100.
258. United States, c. 42, $50-100.

259. Prima, c. 35-38, $250+.

260. Superior, c. 36-40,
$175-250.

261. Schoenhofen-Edelweiss,
c. 36-41, $100-175.

262. Schoenhofen-Edelweiss, c. 36-41, $250+.
263. Schoenhofen-Edelweiss, c. 36-41, $250+.

264. Roosevelt, c. 36-37, $250+.

265. Rock Island, c. 35-39, $250+.

266. Springfield, c. 34-37, $175-250.
267. Springfield, c. 34-37, $100-175.

268. Fortune Bros., c. 46, $100-175.

269. Ruff-Reidel, c. 34-43, $175-250.

270. Springfield, c. 40-45, $250+.

271. Schott, c. L30s-E40s, $250+.

272. Star Union, c. 46, $100-175.
273. Star Union, c. 46, $175-250.
274. Star Union, c. 46, $100-175.

284. Star Union, c. 39, $175-250.

275. Siebens, c. 50, $50-100.

276. Siebens, c. 40s-E50s, $25-50 (f).

277. Peter Fox, c. 40s-E50s, $250+.

278. Springfield, c. 41, $250+.

279. Western, c. 40s, $50-100.

280. Western, c. 47, $100-175.

281. Carling, c. 54-56, $50-100.

282. Springfield, c. 40s-E50s, $250+.

283. Star Union, c. 40s-E50s, $50-100.

285. Star Union, c. 36-39, $175-250.

286. Star Peerless, c. 40s-E50s, $250+.
287. Star Peerless, c. 40s-E50s, $175-250.

290. Birk Bros., c. 35, $250+.

288. Birk Bros., c. 35, $175-250.

291. Birk Bros., c. 35, $250+.

289. Superior, c. 36-40, $175-250.

292. Atlantic, c. 40s-E50s, $250+.
293. Atlantic, c. 40s-E50s, $175-250.
294. Atlantic, c. 40s-E50s, $175-250.

295. Prima, c. 34-41, $175-250.
296. Prima, c. 34-41, $175-250.

297. Prima, c. 34-41, $250+.

298. Koller, c. L30s-40s, $250+.

299. Birk Bros., c. 40s-E50s, $175-250.
300. Birk Bros., c. 40s-E50s, $100-175.

301. Birk Bros., c. 40s-E50s, $100-175.

302. Star Union, c. 36-37, $175-250.

303. Star Union, c. 36-37, $250+.

304. Pilsen, c. 35, $175-250.

305. Peoria, c. L30s-E40s, $250+.

306. Wagner, c. 36-38, $250+.

307. Prima, c. 36-38, $250+.

308. White Eagle, c. 40s-E50s, $175-250.
309. White Eagle, c. 40s-E50s, $175-250.
310. White Eagle, c. 40s-E50s, $175-250.

311. Hoerber, c. 36-41, $175-250.

312. Pilsen, c. 46, $175-250.
313. Pilsen, c. 49, $50-100.
314. Pilsen, c. 49, $50-100.

315. Zeman, c. 42-64, $250+.
316. Zeman, c. 42-64, $250+.

317. Zeman, c. 42-64, $175-250.

Indiana

1935-17
1945-13
1949-12

318. Berghoff, c. 48, $100-175.

319. Berghoff, c. 52, $100-175.

320. Berghoff, c. L30s, $50-100.

321. Terre Haute, c. 40s, $100-175.

322. Terre Haute, c. L30s-40s, $100-175.

323. Terre Haute, c. 40s, $100-175.

324. F. W. Cook, c. 40s-E50s, $100-175.

325. Drewerys, c. 47, $175-250
326. Drewerys, c. 47, $175-250.

327. Drewerys, c. L30s-40s, $175-250.
328. Drewerys, c. L30s-40s, $100-175.

329. Drewerys, c. L30s-40s, $100-175.

330. Ajax, c. 39-41, $250+.

331. South Bend, c. 40s-E50s, $175-250.

332. Kamm & Schellinger, c. 48, $100-175.
333. Kamm & Schellinger, c. 44, $100-175.

334. Kamm & Schellinger, c. L30s-40s, $100-175.
335. Kamm & Schellinger, c. 44, $100-175.

336. Centlivre, c. L40s-E50s, $100-175.
337. Centlivre, c. L40s-E50s, $100-175.

338. Centlivre, c. L40s-E50s, $100-175.

339. Kiley, c. 46, $175-250.
340. Kiley, c. 46, $175-250.
341. Kiley, c. 46, $175-250.

342. K.G.Schmidt, c. L30s-40s, $100-175.

343. Sterling, c. 40s-E50s, $100-175.

344. Sterling, c. 40s-E50s, $100-175.

345. Wm. J. Wittekindt, c. 37-40, $250+.

346. Lafayette, c. L30s-40s, $100-175.

Iowa

1935-4
1945-3
1949-3

347. Blackhawk, c. 44-52,
$175-250.

348. Gateway, c. 40-41, $175-250.
349. Gateway, c. 40-41, $175-250.

350. Zoller, c. 36-44, $175-250.

Kentucky

1935-7
1945-6
1949-6

351. Heidelberg, c. L30s-40s,
$175-250.

352. Bavarian, c. L40s-E50s, $50-100.

353. Bavarian, c. L40s-E50s,
$50-100.

354. Bavarian, c. L40s-E50s, $100-175.
355. Bavarian, c. L40s-E50s, $100-175.

362. Bavarian, c. 45-50, $175-250.

356. Bavarian, c. L40s-E50s, $100-175.
357. Bavarian, c. L40s-E50s, $100-175.

363. Heidelberg, c. L30s-E40s, $100-175.

358. Falls City, c. L30s-E40s, $100-175.

359. Oertel, c. 40s, $50-100.
360. Oertel, c. 40s, $50-100.

364. Geo. Wiedemann, c. L30s-40s, $100-175.

361. Geo. Wiedemann, c. L40s-E50s, $100-175.

Louisiana

1935-7
1945-6
1949-5

365. Jackson, c. 40, $175-250.

Maryland

1935-11
1945-7
1949-7

366. American, c. 40s-E50s, $50-100.

367. American, c. 40s-E50s, $50-100.

368. American, c. 40s-E50s, $50-100.

369. Globe, c. 40, $25-50.
370. Globe, c. 40, $25-50.

371. Free State, c. 40s-E50s, $50-100.

372. Gunthers, c. 39, $50-100.

373. National, c. 36-39, $50-100.
374. National, c. 36-39, $50-100.
375. National, c. 36-39, $50-100.

376. National, c. 36-39, $50-100.
377. National, c. 36-39, $50-100.
378. National, c. 36-39, $50-100.

379. National, c. 36-39, $50-100.
380. National, c. 36-39, $50-100.
381. National, c. 36-39, $50-100.

382. National, c. 36-39, $50-100.

383. Cumberland, c. 46, $50-100.
384. Cumberland, c. 46, $25-50.

385. German, c. 42, $50-100.

386. German, c. 58-69, $50-100.

387. Free State, c. 40s-E50s, $100-175.

Massachusetts

1935-14
1945-13
1949-13

388. Boston Beer, c. 40s-E50s, $100-175.

389. Smith Bros., c. 37-43, $100-175.

390. Enterprise, c. 40s, $100-175.

391. Boston Beer, c. 40s-E50s, $100-175.
392. Boston Beer, c. 40s-E50s, $100-175.
393. Boston Beer, c. 40s-E50s, $100-175.

394. Haffenreffer, c. L30s-40s, $100-175.
395. Haffenreffer, c. L30s-40s, $175-250.

396. Haffenreffer, c. L30s-40s, $100-175.
397. Haffenreffer, c. L30s-40s, $100-175.

398. Brockert, c. 36-39,
$100-175.

399. Brockert, c. 36-39,
$100-175.

400. Harvard, c. 40, $50-100.

401. Croft, c. 40s, $100-175.
402. Croft, c. 40s, $100-175.
403. Croft, c. 40s, $100-175.

410. Croft, c. 40s, $50-100.

404. Croft, c. 39, $50-100.
405. Croft, c. 40s, $50-100.
406. Croft, c. 40s, $100-175.

411. Dawsons, c. 40s-E50s, $100-175.

407. Croft, c. 40s, $100-175.
408. Croft, c. 40s, $100-175.

409. Croft, c. 40s, $100-175.

412. Dawsons, c. 40s-E50s, $100-175.
413. Dawsons, c. 49, $100-175.
414. Dawsons, c. 40s-E50s, $50-100.

415. Dawsons, c. 49, $100-175.
416. Dawsons, c. 40s-E50s, $50-100.

417. Dawsons, c. 40s-E50s, $100-175.
418. Dawsons, c. 40s-E50s, $100-175.

419. Holihan Bros., c. L30s-40s, $100-175.

420. Holihan Bros., c. L30s-40s, $100-175.
421. Holihan Bros., c. L30s-40s, $100-175.

422. Essex, c. 35-38, $175-250.

423. Croft, c. L40s-E50s, $100-175.

429. Cold Spring, c. 46, $100-175.
430. Cold Spring, c. L30s-40s, $50-100.
431. Cold Spring, c. 46, $100-175.

424. Cold Spring, c. 46, $50-100.
425. Cold Spring, c. 46, $50-100.
426. Cold Spring, c. 46, $50-100.

427. Cold Spring, c. L30s-40s, $100-175.
428. Cold Spring, c. L30s-40s, $100-175.

432. Hampden, c. 44, $100-175.

433. Hampden, c. 40s-E50s, $25-50.
434. Hampden, c. 44, $100-175.

435. Hampden, c. 44, $100-175.

436. Hampden, c. 44, $175-250.

437. Hampden, c. 40s-E50s, $25-50.
438. Hampden, c. 40s-E50s, $25-50.

439. Harvard, c. 40s-E50s, $50-100.
440. Harvard, c. 40s-E50s, $100-175.
441. Harvard, c. 40s-E50s, $50-100.

442. Harvard, c. 40s-E50s, $50-100.
443. Harvard, c. 40s-E50s, $50-100.

444. Harvard, c. 40s-E50s, $50-100.
445. Harvard, c. 40s-E50s, $50-100.

446. Diamond Spring, c. 41, $50-100.
447. Diamond Spring, c. 41, $50-100.
448. Diamond Spring, c. 41, $50-100.

449. Diamond Spring, c. 41, $50-100.

450. Diamond Spring, c. 41, $50-100.

451. Diamond Spring, c. 41, $100-175.
452. Diamond Spring, c. 40, $100-175.

453. Sullivan, c. L30s, $250+.

456. Springfield, c. 46-48, $100-175.

460. Enterprise, c. 40s, $100-175.

454. Star, c. 39, $100-175.

457. Enterprise, c. 40s, $50-100.
458. Enterprise, c. 40s, $100-175.

455. Star, c. 39, $100-175.

459. Worcester, c. 50s, $100-175.

461. Haffenreffer, c. 40s, $25-50.
462. Haffenreffer, c. 40s, $25-50.
463. Haffenreffer, c. 40s, $25-50.

464. Haffenreffer, c. 40s, $50-100.
465. Haffenreffer, c. 40s, $100-175.
466. Haffenreffer, c. 40s, $50-100.

467. Croft, c. 40s, $100-175.

468. Croft, c. 40s, $100-175.

469. Smith Bros., c. 37-43, $175-250.

470. Star, c. 40s, $100-175.

471. Star, c. 40s, $100-175.
472. Star, c. 40s, $100-175.

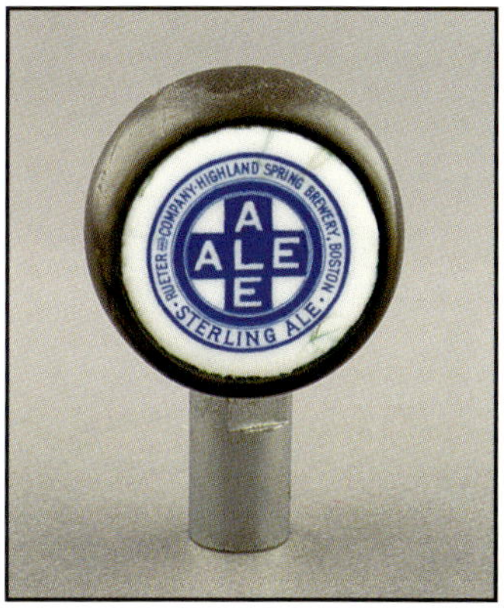

473. Highland Spring, c. 33-36, $250+.

475. Tivoli, c. L30s-E40s, $100-175.
476. Tivoli, c. L30s-E40s, $100-175.
477. Tivoli, c. 48, $100-175.

Michigan

1935-45
1945-23
1949-21

474. Tivoli, c. L30s-E40s, $100-175.

478. Auto City, c. 35-43, $250+.

479. Bosch, c. L40s-E50s, $100-175.

480. Bosch, c. L40s-E50s, $100-175.

481. Michigan, c. 37, $100-175.

482. Food City, c. 36-40, $100-175.

483. American, c. 36-37, $175-250.

484. Zynda, c. 36-38, $250+.

485. Detroit, c. 36, $250+.

486. E & B, c. 55, $100-175.

487. E & B, c. E50s, $175-250.
488. E & B, c. E50s, $100-175.

489. E & B, c. E50s, $100-175.
490. E & B, c. E50s, $100-175.
491. E & B, c. E50s, $100-175.

492. Bay City, c. 46-50, $250+.

493. Fox Deluxe, c. 50-53, $100-175.

494. Frankenmuth, c. 40s, $175-250.
495. Frankenmuth, c. 40s, $175-250.

503. Goebel, c. 40s-E50s, $250+.

496. Frankenmuth, c. 40s, $25-50 (f).

504. Goebel, c. 40s-E50s, $100-175.

497. Frankenmuth, c. 40s, $175-250.
498. Frankenmuth, c. 40s, $175-250.
499. Frankenmuth, c. 40s, $175-250.

500. Grand Valley, c. 36-37, $250+.

501. Grand Valley, c. 36-37, $250+.

502. Geyer Bros., c. 40s-E50s, $175-250.

505. Goebel, c. 40s-E50s, $100-175.
506. Goebel, c. 40s-E50s, $100-175.
507. Goebel, c. 40s-E50s, $50-100.

508. Eberle, c. 36-41, $100-175.

509. A. A. Haas, c. 41, $100-175.

510. Kings Tavern, c. 38-39, $250+.

511. PH. Kling, c. L30s-E40s, $175-250.

512. Kolb, c. 36-43, $175-250.

513. Koppitz-Melchers, c. L30s-E40s, $100-175.
514. Koppitz-Melchers, c. L30s-E40s, $100-175.

515. Detroit, c. 41-48, $175-250.

516. Menominee-Marinette, c. 40s, $100-175.

517. Sebewaing, c. 38-45, $250+.

518. Sebewaing, c. 38-45, $175-250.
519. Sebewaing, c. 38-45, $175-250.

520. Detroit, c. 35-48, $175-250.
521. Detroit, c. 35-48, $100-175.

525. Pfeiffer, c. E50s, $100-175.

526. Phoenix, c. 35-39, $250+.

527. Schmidt's, c. L30s-40s, $100-175.
528. Schmidt's, c. L30s-40s, $100-175.
529. Schmidt's, c. L30s-40s, $100-175.

522. Pfeiffer, c. E50s, $100-175.
523. Pfeiffer, c. E50s, $100-175.
524. Pfeiffer, c. E50s, $100-175.

530. Silver Foam, c. 34-40, $175-250.

531. Detroit, c. 40-48, $175-250.

532. Soo, c. 41, $175-250.
533. Soo, c. 41, $175-250.

534. Stroh, c. L30s, $175-250.

535. Stroh, c. L30s, $100-175.
536. Stroh, c. L30s, $100-175.

537. Tivoli, c. 36-44, $100-175.

Minnesota

1935-24
1945-19
1949-19

538. Duluth, c. L30s-40s, $100-175.

539. Cold Spring, c. 40s, $100-175.

540. Fitger, c. 40s-E50s, $175-250.
541. Fitger, c. 38, $100-175.
542. Fitger, c. 40s-E50s, $100-175.

543. Glueck, c. 40s-E50s, $100-175.
544. Glueck, c. 40s-E50s, $175-250.

548. Theo Hamm, c. 36, $175-250.
549. Theo Hamm, c. 36, $175-250.
550. Theo Hamm, c. 36, $100-175.

545. Minneapolis, c. 46-56, $250+.
546. Minneapolis, c. 46-56, $100-175.
547. Minneapolis, c. 46-56, $175-250.

551. Theo Hamm, c. 36, $175-250.
552. Theo Hamm, c. 51, $100-175.

561. Jacob Schmidt, c. 47, $100-175.
562. Jacob Schmidt, c. 40s-E50s, $175-250.

553. Duluth, c. 35-44, $175-250.

556. Premier, c. 36, $250+.

554. Kiewel, c. 40s-E50s, $50-100.

557. Jacob Schmidt, c. 55-62, $100-175.

555. Peoples, c. L30s-40s, $250+.

558. Jacob Schmidt, c. 49, $175-250.
559. Jacob Schmidt, c. 51, $50-100.
560. Jacob Schmidt, c. 49, $175-250.

Missouri

1935-21
1945-12
1949-8

563. Columbia, c. L40s, $100-175.

564. Anheuser-Busch, c. L30s, $175-250.

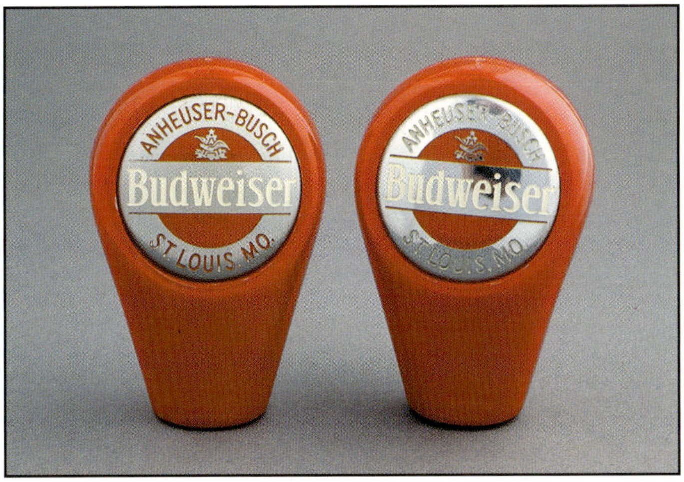

565. Anheuser-Busch, c. L30s, $50-100.
566. Anheuser-Busch, c. L30s, $50-100.

567. Anheuser-Busch, c. L30s, $100-175.
568. Anheuser-Busch, c. 40s, $50-100.
569. Anheuser-Busch, c. 48, $50-100.

570. Anheuser-Busch, c. 36-38, $250+.

571. Peerless, c. 34-40, $250+.

572. M. K. Goetz, c. 40s-E50s, $100-175.
573. M. K. Goetz, c. 40s-E50s, $100-175.

574. M. K. Goetz, c. 40s-E50s, $175-250.
575. M. K. Goetz, c. 40s-E50s, $50-100.
576. M. K. Goetz, c. 40s-E50s, $100-175.

577. Falstaff, c. 49, $50-100.
578. Falstaff, c. 49, $50-100.
579. Falstaff, c. 33, $50-100.

580. Gast, c. 34-46, $175-250.

581. Griesedieck Bros., c. 40s-E50s, $100-175.

582. Griesedieck Bros., c. 40s-E50s, $175-250.
583. Griesedieck Bros., c. 52-59, $25-50.
584. Griesedieck Bros., c. 52-59, $100-175.

585. Hyde Park, c. 40s, $175-250.

586. Hyde Park, c. 40s, $100-175.
587. Hyde Park, c. 40s, $100-175.

588. Hyde Park, c. 40s, $100-175.
589. Hyde Park, c. 40s, $100-175.
590. Hyde Park, c. 40s, $175-250.

591. Anheuser-Busch, c. 48, $50-100.
592. Anheuser-Busch, c. 30s, $100-175.
593. Anheuser-Busch, c. 30s, $100-175.

594. Anheuser-Busch, c. 30s, $100-175.
595. Anheuser-Busch, c. 52, $50-100.
596. Anheuser-Busch, c. 30s, $50-100.

597. George Muehlebach, c. 40s-E50s, $100-175.

598. George Muehlebach, c. 40s-E50s, $175-250.
599. George Muehlebach, c. 40s-E50s, $100-175.

600. Anheuser-Busch, c. 30s, $250+.

601. Western, c. 40s, $50-100.

Montana

1935-10
1945-8
1949-8

602. Butte, c. 40s-E50s, $175-250.

603. Sicks Great Falls, c. 45-49, $175-250.
604. Sicks Great Falls, c. 45-49, $175-250.

605. Missoula, c. 40s-E50s, $175-250.
606. Missoula, c. 40s-E50s, $175-250.
607. Missoula, c. 40s-E50s, $175-250.

608. Missoula, c. 40s-E50s, $175-250.
609. Missoula, c. 41, $250+.

Nebraska

1935-5
1945-4
1949-4

610. Crete, c. 36-41, $175-250.

611. Metz, c. 40s, $175-250.
612. Fontenelle, c. 36-38, $175-250.
613. Metz, c. 40s, $175-250.

614. Fontenelle, c. 34-38, $250+.

615. Columbus, c. E50s, $250+.

616. Storz, c. 40s-E50s, $100-175.

Nevada

1935-2
1945-2
1949-1

617. Reno, c. 49, $250+.

618. Reno, c. 40s-E50s, $250+.

New Hampshire

1935-1
1945-1
1949-1

619. Frank Jones, c. 40s-E50s, $100-175.
620. Frank Jones, c. 40s-E50s, $100-175.

621. Eldredge, c. 36-40, $100-175.

New Jersey

1935-15
1945-12
1949-11

622. Wm. Peter, c. 36, $100-175.

623. Wm. Peter, c. 36, $100-175.
624. Wm. Peter, c. 36, $100-175.
625. Wm. Peter, c. 36, $50-100.

626. P. Ballantine, c. L30s, $50-100.
627. P. Ballantine, c. L30s, $1-25.
628. P. Ballantine, c. L30s, $1-25.

629. P. Ballantine, c. L30s, $1-25.
630. P. Ballantine, c. L30s, $25-50.
631. P. Ballantine, c. L40s, $50-100.

632. P. Ballantine, c. 40s-E50s, $50-100.
633. P. Ballantine, c. 40s-E50s, $50-100.
634. P. Ballantine, c. 40s-E50s, $25-50.

635. P. Ballantine, c. E50s, $25-50.
636. P. Ballantine, c. 40s-E50s, $25-50 (f).

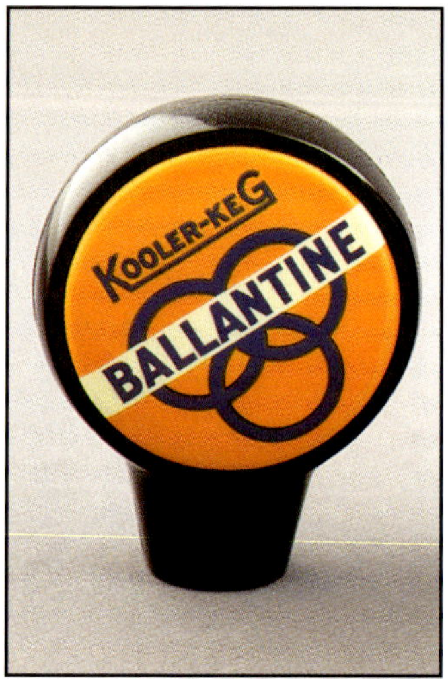

637. P. Ballantine, c. L30s, $1-25.

638. Peter Breidt, c. L30s, $25-50.
639. Peter Breidt, c. L30s, $25-50 (f).
640. Peter Breidt, c. L30s, $25-50.

641. Peter Breidt, c. 42, $25-50.
642. Peter Breidt, c. 42, $25-50.

643. Peter Breidt, c. 35-51, $25-50.

644. Burton, c. 34-40, $100-175.
645. Burton, c. 34-40, $100-175.

646. Camden County, c. 42, $100-175.
647. Camden County, c. 40s, $100-175.
648. Camden County, c. 42, $100-175.

649. New Brunswick, c. 35-38, $175-250.

650. Christian Feigenspan, c. 39, $50-100.
651. Christian Feigenspan, c. 39, $50-100.

652. Christian Feigenspan, c. 39, $50-100.
653. Christian Feigenspan, c. 39, $50-100.
654. Christian Feigenspan, c. 39, $100-175.

655. Burton, c. 36-49, $100-175.
656. Burton, c. 36-49, $100-175.
657. Burton, c. 36-49, $100-175.

658. Burton, c. 36-49, $100-175.

659. Jos. Hensler, c. 40s, $50-100.
660. Jos. Hensler, c. 36, $50-100.

661. Jos. Hensler, c. 35, $100-175.
662. Jos. Hensler, c. 36, $50-100.
663. Jos. Hensler, c. 35, $100-175.

664. Jos. Hensler, c. 35, $100-175.
665. Jos. Hensler, c. 35, $50-100.

666. Hoffman, c. 34-46, $100-175.
667. Hoffman, c. 34-46, $100-175.
668. Hoffman, c. 34-46, $100-175.

669. Eastern, c. 51, $50-100.
670. Eastern, c. 51, $100-175.
671. Eastern, c. 51, $50-100.

672. New Brunswick, c. 35-38, $175-250.
673. New Brunswick, c. 35-38, $175-250.
674. New Brunswick, c. 35-38, $175-250.

675. Eastern, c. L40s, $100-175.

676. Peoples, c. 40s-E50s, $175-250.

677. G. Krueger, c. 52, $100-175.

678. G. Krueger, c. L40s, $50-100.
679. G. Krueger, c. L40s, $50-100.

680. G. Krueger, c. 40s-E50s, $25-50.
681. G. Krueger, c. 40s-E50s, $50-100.
682. G. Krueger, c. 40s-E50s, $25-50 (f).

683. G. Krueger, c. 40s-E50s, $50-100.
684. G. Krueger, c. 40s-E50s, $50-100.
685. G. Krueger, c. 40s-E50s, $50-100.

686. G. Krueger, c. 40s-E50s, $25-50.
687. G. Krueger, c. 40s-E50s, $50-100.
688. G. Krueger, c. 40s-E50s, $25-50.

689. G. Krueger, c. 40s-E50s, $50-100.
690. G. Krueger, c. 40s-E50s, $50-100.
691. G. Krueger, c. 40s-E50s, $50-100.

692. G. Krueger, c. 40s-E50s, $25-50 (f).
693. G. Krueger, c. 40s-E50s, $25-50 (f).
694. G. Krueger, c. 40s-E50s, $25-50 (f).

695. G. Krueger, c. 40s-E50s, $50-100.
696. G. Krueger, c. 40s-E50s, $50-100.
697. G. Krueger, c. 40s-E50s, $50-100.

698. Peter Doelger, c. 35-48, $175-250.

699. Camden County, c. 40s, $175-250.

700. Burton, c. 42, $50-100.
701. Burton, c. 42, $50-100.
702. Burton, c. 42, $50-100.

703. Eastern, c. 40s, $175-250.

704. Peoples, c. 36-49, $100-175.
705. Peoples, c. 36-49, $100-175.

706. Wm. Peter, c. 45, $175-250.

707. Wm. Peter, c. 45, $175-250.
708. Wm. Peter, c. 45, $175-250.
709. Wm. Peter, c. 45, $175-250.

710. Wm. Peter, c. 45, $175-250.
711. Wm. Peter, c. 45, $175-250.
712. Wm. Peter, c. 45, $175-250.

713. Wm. Peter, c. 45, $175-250.
714. Wm. Peter, c. 45, $175-250.

715. Peter Doelger, c. 35-48, $100-175.

716. Peter Doelger, c. 35-48, $100-175.
717. Peter Doelger, c. 35-48, $100-175.
718. Peter Doelger, c. 35-48, $100-175.

719. Peter Doelger, c. 35-48, $100-175.
720. Peter Doelger, c. 35-48, $100-175.
721. Peter Doelger, c. 35-48, $100-175.

722. Peter Doelger, c. 35-48, $100-175.

723. Sprattler & Mennel, c. 39-40, $175-250.

724. Schultz, c. 35-45, $175-250.
725. Schultz, c. 35-45, $175-250.
726. Schultz, c. 35-45, $175-250.

727. Schultz, c. 35-45, $175-250.
728. Burton, c. 35-45, $175-250.
729. Burton, c. 35-45, $175-250.

730. Seeber, c. 34-38, $175-250.

732. Peoples, c. 37-49, $175-250.

731. Peoples, c. 37-49, $175-250.

733. Union, c. 34, $175-250.

734. Burton, c. 36-49, $175-250.
735. Burton, c. 36-49, $175-250.

736. Burton, c. 36-49, $175-250.
737. Burton, c. 36-49, $175-250.

New Mexico

1935-0
1945-0
1949-0

738. Rio Grande, c. 37-39, $250+.

New York

1935-69
1945-44
1949-34

739. Amsterdam, c. 34-38, $250+.

740. Amsterdam, c. 34-38, $250+.

741. American, c. 40, $175-250.

745. Greater New York, c. 46-50, $175-250.
746. Greater New York, c. 46-50, $100-175.

747. Bartels, c. 38, $100-175

748. Bartels, c. 38, $100-175.

742. Peter Barmann, c. 36-41, $175-250.
743. Peter Barmann, c. 36-41, $100-175.
744. Peter Barmann, c. 36-41, $175-250.

749. Magnus Beck, c. 40s, $50-100.
750. Magnus Beck, c. 40s, $25-50.
751. Magnus Beck, c. 40s, $50-100.

757. Haberle Congress, c. 38, $50-100.

752. Beverwyck, c. 40s-E50s, $25-50.
753. Beverwyck, c. 40s-E50s, $25-50.

758. Haberle Congress, c. 39-50, $100-175.

754. Beverwyck, c. 41, $25-50.

759. Old Dutch, c. 35-48, $250+.

755. Beverwyck, c. 48, $25-50.
756. Beverwyck, c. 49, $25-50.

760. Kings, c. L30s, $250+.
761. Kings, c. L30s, $250+.

762. Burke, c. 34-45, $100-175.

763. Burke, c. 41, $50-100.
764. Burke, c. 41, $50-100.

765. Burke, c. 41, $50-100.
766. Burke, c. 41, $100-175.
767. Burke, c. 41, $100-175.

768. George F. Stein, c. 52, $50-100.
769. George F. Stein, c. 52, $50-100.
770. George F. Stein, c. 52, $50-100.

771. George F. Stein, c. 46, $100-175.
772. George F. Stein, c. 46, $100-175.

773. Cataract, c. 40, $100-175.
774. Cataract, c. 40, $100-175.

775. George F. Stein, c. 46-57, $100-175.
776. George F. Stein, c. 46, $100-175.
777. George F. Stein, c. 46-57, $100-175.

778. Chautauqua, c. 39-41, $175-250.

779. Frontier, c. 35-48, $50-100.
780. Frontier, c. 35-48, $50-100.

781. Cataract, c. 36-40, $100-175.

782. Haberle Congress, c. L30s, $50-100.

783. Deerpark Beverages, c. 34-41, $175-250.

784. Haberle Congress, c. 42, $100-175.

785. Genesee, c. 56-58, $175-250.

786. Dobler, c. 40, $25-50.
787. Dobler, c. 40, $25-50.
788. Dobler, c. 40, $25-50.

789. Dobler, c. 40, $25-50.

792. North American, c. 40, $100-175.
793. North American, c. 40, $50-100.

797. Hendrick, c. 40s-E50s, $50-100.

790. Dobler, c. 40s-E50s, $50-100.
791. Dobler, c. 40s-E50s, $25-50.

794. Chas. Schaefer, c. 46-48, $100-175.
795. Chas. Schaefer, c. 46-48, $100-175.
796. North American, c. L30s-E40s, $100-175.

798. Hendrick, c. 40s-E50s, $50-100.
799. Hendrick, c. 36, $50-100.

800. Geo. F. Stein, c. 40s-E50s,
$175-250.

801. Empire State, c. 38, $100-175.
802. Empire State, c. 38, $100-175.

803. Empire State, c. 38,
$50-100.

804. Van Buren, c. 40-47, $100-175.
805. Van Buren, c. 42, $50-100.
806. Van Buren, c. 40-47, $175-250.

807. Deerpark Beverages,
c. 34-41, $250+

809. Ebling, c. 42-51, $25-50.

808. Eagle, c. 36-43, $175-250.

810. Ebling, c. 42-51, $100-175.
811. Ebling, c. 42, $100-175.
812. Ebling, c. 46, $100-175.

813. Ebling, c. 46, $100-175.
814. Ebling, c. 46, $50-100.
815. Ebling, c. 46, $50-100.

816. Edelbrau, c. 46-51, $100-175.
817. Edelbrau, c. 46-51, $100-175.
818. Edelbrau, c. 40-46, $100-175.

819. Edelbrau, c. 46-51, $50-100.
820. Edelbrau, c. 46-51, $100-175.
821. Edelbrau, c. 46-51, $50-100.

822. Edelbrau, c. 46-51, $50-100.
823. Edelbrau, c. 46-51, $100-175.
824. Goldenrod, c. 46-51, $100-175.

825. Edelbrew, c. 46-51, $25-50.
826. Edelbrew, c. 46-51, $50-100.
827. Edelbrew, c. 46-51, $25-50.

828. Edelbrew, c. 46-51, $50-100.

829. Geo. Ehret, c. L30s, $100-175.
830. Geo. Ehret, c. L30s, $100-175.

831. Geo. Ehret, c. L40s, $100-175.
832. Geo. Ehret, c. L30s, $100-175.
833. Geo. Ehret, c. L40s, $100-175.

834. Geo. Ehret, c. L40s, $100-175.
835. Geo. Ehret, c. L40s, $100-175.
836. Geo. Ehret, c. L40s, $100-175.

837. John Eichler, c. L30s-E40s, $50-100.

838. Nectar, c. 35-37, $250+.

839. Nectar, c. 35-37, $250+.

840. Empire State, c. 34-40, $175-250.

841. Peter Barmann, c. 36, $250+.

842. Fidelio, c. 38, $50-100.

843. Fitzgerald, c. 53, $25-50.

844. Fitzgerald, c. 35, $25-50.

845. Fitzgerald, c. 35, $100-175.

846. Fitzgerald, c. 40s-E50s, $25-50.
847. Fitzgerald, c. 40s-E50s, $25-50.
848. Fitzgerald, c. 40s-E50s, $25-50.

852. Utica, c. 40s, $50-100.
853. Utica, c. 40s, $50-100.
854. Utica, c. 40s, $100-175.

855. Utica, c. 40s, $100-175.

856. Fort Stanwix, c. 35-37,
$175-250.

849. Fitzgerald, c. 40s-E50s,
$25-50.

850. Fitzgerald, c. 40s-E50s, $50-100.
851. Fitzgerald, c. 35, $50-100.

857. Genesee, c. 40s-E50s, $100-175.
858. Genesee, c. 48, $100-175.
859. Genesee, c. 40s-E50s, $50-100.

860. Genesee, c. 48, $50-100.
861. Genesee, c. 51, $1-25.
862. Genesee, c. 48, $25-50.

863. Genesee, c. 48, $50-100.

864. Genesee, c. 40s-E50s, $25-50.

865. Genesee, c. 51, $25-50.
866. Genesee, c. 51, $1-25.
867. Genesee, c. 51, $25-50.

868. Lion, c. 36-41, $100-175.

869. Edelbrau, c. L30s-E40s, $100-175.
870. Edelbrau, c. L30s-E40s, $100-175.
871. Edelbrau, c. L30s, $100-175.

872. Edelbrau, c. 40-46, $175-250.
873. Edelbrau, c. 40-46, $175-250.

874. Greater New York, c. 46-50, $175-250.

878. Greenway, c. L30s-40s, $175-250.

879. Greenway, c. L30s-40s, $100-175.

880. Haberle Congress, c. L40s, $100-175.

881. Hendrick, c. 46, $50-100.

882. Hendrick, c. 38, $50-100.

883. Hendrick, c. 37, $175-250.

875. Greenway, c. L30s-40s, $100-175.
876. Greenway, c. L30s-40s, $100-175.
877. Greenway, c. L30s-40s, $100-175.

884. Ebling, c. 36-37, $25-50 (f).

885. Hornell, c. 40s-E50s, $50-100.

890. Horton Pilsener, c. 36-40, $175-250.
891. Horton Pilsener, c. 36-40, $50-100.
892. Horton Pilsener, c. 36-40, $175-250.

886. Gerhard Lang, c. 44-49, $100-175.
887. Gerhard Lang, c. 44-49, $100-175.

893. Horton Pilsener, c. 36-40, $50-100.

888. Gerhard Lang, c. 44-49, $100-175.

889. Gerhard Lang, c. 44-49, $100-175.

894. J Chr G. Hupfel, c. 36-38, $175-250.

895. North American, c. L30s-E40s, $100-175.

896. North American, c. L30s-E40s, $50-100.
897. Chas. Schaefer, c. 46-48, $50-100.
898. North American, c. L30s-E40s, $50-100.

899. Moore & Quinn, c. L30s-40s, $100-175.

900. Iroquois, c. L30s, $50-100.

901. Iroquois, c. L30s, $100-175.

902. Northern, c. L30s-E40s, $250+.

903. Edelbrew, c. 46-57, $250+.

904. Hornell, c. 40s, $50-100.

905. Kips Bay, c. 34-37, $175-250.
906. Kips Bay, c. 34-37, $175-250.

907. Kips Bay, c. L40s, $175-250.

908. Kips Bay, c. L40s, $175-250.

909. Kips Bay, c. L40s, $175-250.

910. Fred Koch, c. 38, $50-100.

911. Fred Koch, c. 39, $25-50 (f).

912. City, c. 46-50, $100-175.

913. Gerhard Lang, c. 41, $100-175.

914. Gerhard Lang, c. 41, $50-100.
915. Gerhard Lang, c. 41, $50-100.
916. Gerhard Lang, c. 41, $50-100.

917. Liebmann, c. 36-39, $100-175.
918. Liebmann, c. 36-39, $100-175.

919. Linden, c. 38-47, $175-250.
920. Linden, c. 38-47, $175-250.

921. Linden, c. 41, $175-250.
922. Linden, c. 41, $175-250.
923. Linden, c. 38-47, $175-250.

924. Lion, c. 36-41, $100-175.

925. Lion, c. 36-41, $100-175.
926. Lion, c. 36-41, $100-175.
927. Lion, c. 36-41, $100-175.

928. Lion, c. 36-41, $100-175.
929. Lion, c. 36-41, $100-175.

930. Loewers, c. L30s-E40s, $100-175.
931. Loewers, c. L30s-E40s, $100-175.

932. Loewers, c. L30s-E40s, $175-250.
933. Loewers, c. L30s-E40s, $175-250.

934. Frontier, c. L40s, $100-175.
935. Frontier, c. L40s, $100-175.
936. Frontier, c. L40s, $100-175.

937. Schreiber, c. 43, $100-175.

938. Schreiber, c. 40s-E50s, $50-100.
939. Schreiber, c. 40s-E50s, $50-100.
940. Schreiber, c. 40s-E50s, $50-100.

941. West End, c. 54, $50-100.

946. Fidelio, c. 37, $100-175.

949. Moore & Quinn, c. 44, $100-175.

942. McCoy, c. 54-57, $100-175.

947. Phoenix, c. 40s, $50-100.
948. Phoenix, c. 40s, $100-175.

950. Old Dutch, c. 35-48, $50-100.

943. Fidelio, c. 37, $100-175.
944. Fidelio, c. 37, $100-175.
945. Fidelio, c. 37, $100-175.

951. Old Dutch, c. L30s-E40s, $100-175.
952. Old Dutch, c. L30s-E40s, $100-175.

962. Jacob Ruppert, c. 40s-E50s, $50-100.
963. Jacob Ruppert, c. 40s-E50s, $50-100.
964. Jacob Ruppert, c. 40s-E50s, $50-100.

953. Cataract, c. 36-40, $100-175.

956. Empire State, c. 36-40, $175-250.

965. Empire State, c. 36-40, $175-250.

966. Horton Pilsener, c. 36-40, $175-250.

954. West End, c. 40s-E50s, $50-100.

957. Phoenix, c. 36-45, $100-175.
958. Phoenix, c. 36-45, $100-175.

967. Standard, c. 40s-E50s, $100-175.

955. Gerhard Lang, c. 36-49, $50-100.

959. Liebmann, c. 36-38, $175-250.
960. Liebmann, c. 36-38, $100-175.
961. Liebmann, c. 36-38, $175-250.

968. Hornell, c. 42, $50-100.
969. Hornell, c. 42, $50-100.

970. Horton, c. 36-40, $100-175.

971. Genesee, c. 36-40, $175-250.

972. Rochester, c. 50, $50-100.

973. Rochester, c. 50, $50-100.
974. Rochester, c. 50, $50-100.
975. Rochester, c. 50, $100-175.

976. Rochester, c. 50, $100-175.
977. Rochester, c. 50, $100-175.

978. Stanton, c. 40s-E50s, $100-175.

979. Oneida, c. 36-39, $175-250.

980. Rochester, c. 36-43, $175-250.

981. North American, c. L30s-E40s, $100-175.

982. Phoenix, c. 40s-E50s, $100-175.
983. Phoenix, c. 40s-E50s, $50-100.
984. Phoenix, c. 40s-E50s, $100-175.

985. Phoenix, c. 40s-E50s, $100-175.

986. Piel Bros., c. 40s-E50s, $25-50.
987. Piel Bros., c. 40s-E50s, $50-100.
988. Piel Bros., c. 40s-E50s, $25-50.

989. Piel Bros., c. 40s-E50s, $25-50.
990. Piel Bros., c. 40s-E50s, $25-50.
991. Piel Bros., c. 40s-E50s, $50-100.

992. Piel Bros., c. 40s-E50s, $100-175.
993. Piel Bros., c. 40s-E50s, $25-50.
994. Piel Bros., c. 40s-E50s, $25-50.

995. Piel Bros., c. 40s-E50s, $50-100.
996. Piel Bros., c. 40s-E50s, $100-175.
997. Piel Bros., c. 40s-E50s, $100-175.

998. Piel Bros., c. 40s-E50s, $25-50.
999. Piel Bros., c. 40s-E50s, $25-50.

1000. Piel Bros., c. 40s-E50s, $100-175.
1001. Piel Bros., c. 40s-E50s, $100-175.

1002. Pillser, c. L30s-E40s, $50-100.
1003. Pilser, c. L30s-E40s, $50-100.
1004. Pilser, c. L30s-E40s, $100-175.

1005. Pilser, c. L30s-E40s, $100-175.
1006. Pilser, c. L30s-E40s, $100-175.

1007. Power City, c. 37-40, $250+.

1008. Quandt, c. 36-41, $100-175.

1009. Quandt, c. 36-41, $100-175.

1010. Moore & Quinn, c. L30s-40s, $100-175.

1011. Rubsam & Horrmann, c. 46, $50-100.
1012. Rubsam & Horrmann, c. 46, $50-100.
1013. Rubsam & Horrmann, c. 47, $50-100.

1023. Liebmann, c. 40s-E50s, $50-100.
1024. Liebmann, c. 40s-E50s, $50-100.
1025. Liebmann, c. 40s-E50s, $50-100.

1014. Rubsam & Horrmann, c. 46, $100-175.
1015. Rubsam & Horrmann, c. 46, $50-100.
1016. Rubsam & Horrmann, c. 46, $25-50.

1026. Liebmann, c. 40s-E50s, $100-175.

1017. Rubsam & Horrmann, c. L30s, $25-50.
1018. Rubsam & Horrmann, c. L30s, $50-100.
1019. Rubsam & Horrmann, c. 47, $25-50.

1027. Liebmann, c. 40s-E50s, $50-100.
1028. Liebmann, c. 40s-E50s, $50-100.
1029. Liebmann, c. 40s-E50s, $50-100.

1020. Rubsam & Horrmann, c. 47, $50-100.
1021. Rubsam & Horrmann, c. L30s, $25-50.
1022. Rubsam & Horrmann, c. L30s, $50-100.

1030. Liebmann, c. 40s-E50s, $100-175.
1031. Liebmann, c. 40s-E50s, $100-175.

1032. Liebmann, c. 40s-E50s, $1-25.
1033. Liebmann, c. 40s-E50s, $50-100.
1034. Liebmann, c. 40s-E50s, $50-100.

1035. Goldenrod, c. 42-44, $100-175.

1036. Edelbrau, c. 42-44, $100-175.
1037. Edelbrau, c. 42-44, $100-175.

1038. Jacob Ruppert, c. 38-51, $25-50.
1039. Jacob Ruppert, c. L30s-40s, $25-50.
1040. Jacob Ruppert, c. L30s-40s, $25-50.

1041. Jacob Ruppert, c. L30s-40s, $25-50.
1042. Jacob Ruppert, c. L30s-40s, $25-50.
1043. Jacob Ruppert, c. L30s-40s, $25-50.

1044. Jacob Ruppert, c. L30s-40s, $25-50.
1045. Jacob Ruppert, c. L30s-40s, $25-50.
1046. Jacob Ruppert, c. L30s-40s, $25-50.

1047. Jacob Ruppert, c. L30s-40s, $25-50.
1048. Jacob Ruppert, c. L30s-40s, $25-50.
1049. Jacob Ruppert, c. L30s-40s, $25-50.

1050. Jacob Ruppert, c. L30s-40s, $25-50.
1051. Jacob Ruppert, c. L30s-40s, $25-50.
1052. Jacob Ruppert, c. L30s-40s, $25-50.

1053. Jacob Ruppert, c. L30s-40s, $50-100.

1054. Jacob Ruppert, c. L30s-40s, $50-100.
1055. Jacob Ruppert, c. L30s-40s, $25-50.

1060. Schreiber, c. 35-50, $100-175.
1061. Schreiber, c. 35-50, $100-175.

1062. Hornell, c. 36, $100-175.
1063. Hornell, c. 36, $100-175.

1056. Amsterdam, c. 36, $250+.

1057. F & M Schaefer, c. 40s-E50s, $25-50.
1058. F & M Schaefer, c. 40s-E50s, $50-100.
1059. F & M Schaefer, c. 40s-E50s, $25-50.

1064. Liebmann, c. 37, $50-100.
1065. Liebmann, c. 37, $50-100.

1076. Standard, c. 40s-E50s, $100-175.
1077. Standard, c. 40s-E50s, $50-100.

1066. Nectar, c. 36-38, $250+.

1071. Wm. Simon, c. L30s, $25-50.
1072. Wm. Simon, c. L30s, $25-50.

1067. Deerpark, c. 30s, $250+.

1073. Kips Bay, c. L40s, $175-250.
1074. Greater New York, c. L40s, $175-250.
1075. Kips Bay, c. L40s, $175-250.

1068. Wm. Simon, c. L30s, $25-50.
1069. Wm. Simon, c. L30s, $100-175.
1070. Wm. Simon, c. L30s, $25-50.

1078. Standard, c. 40s-E50s, $50-100.
1079. Standard, c. 40s-E50s, $50-100.
1080. Standard, c. 40s-E50s, $50-100.

1087. Geo. F. Stein, c. 40s-E50s, $100-175.
1088. Geo. F. Stein, c. 48, $100-175.
1089. Geo. F. Stein, c. 48, $50-100.

1081. Stanton, c. L30s-40s, $50-100.
1082. Stanton, c. L30s-40s, $50-100.
1083. Stanton, c. L30s-40s, $50-100.

1090. Geo. F. Stein, c. 48, $50-100.
1091. Geo. F. Stein, c. 48, $100-175.

1084. Stanton, c. L30s-40s, $50-100.
1085. Stanton, c. L30s-40s, $50-100.

1086. Ebling, c. L30s-E40s, $100-175.

1092. Standard, c. 40s-E50s, $100-175.

1093. City, c. 39, $100-175.
1094. City, c. 39, $100-175.

1095. City, c. 39, $100-175.
1096. City, c. 39, $100-175.

1097. American, c. 40s-E50s, $50-100.
1098. American, c. 40s-E50s, $100-175.
1099. American, c. 40s-E50s, $100-175.

1100. American, c. 40s-E50s, $50-100.
1101. American, c. 40s-E50s, $50-100.
1102. American, c. 40s-E50s, $50-100.

1103. American, c. 40s-E50s,
$100-175.

1104. American, c. 40s-E50s, $100-175.
1105. American, c. 40s-E50s, $100-175.

1106. Rochester, c. 40s-E50s, $50-100.
1107. Rochester, c. 40s-E50s, $100-175.

1108. John F. Trommer, c. L30s-E40s, $50-100.
1109. John F. Trommer, c. L30s-E40s, $25-50.

1110. John F. Trommer, c. L30s-40s, $25-50 (f).
1111. John F. Trommer, c. L30s-40s, $50-100.

1112. John F. Trommer, c. L30s-E40s, $25-50.
1113. John F. Trommer, c. L30s-40s, $50-100.
1114. John F. Trommer, c. L30s-E40s, $25-50.

1115. John F. Trommer, c. L30s-40s, $50-100.
1116. John F. Trommer, c. L30s-E40s, $50-100.
1117. John F. Trommer, c. L30s-E40s, $50-100.

1118. John F. Trommer, c. L30s-E40s, $100-175.

1119. Old Dutch, c. L30s-E40s, $175-250.

1120. West End, c. L30s, $100-175.
1121. West End, c. L30s, $100-175.
1122. West End, c. L30s, $100-175.

1123. West End, c. 40s, $100-175.
1124. West End, c. 40s, $100-175.
1125. West End, c. L30s, $50-100.

1126. West End, c. 40s, $100-175.
1127. West End, c. 40s, $25-50.
1128. West End, c. 40s, $25-50.

1129. West End, c. 30s, $25-50.

1130. Lion, c. 36-41, $100-175.
1131. Greater New York, c. 46-50, $100-175.
1132. Lion, c. 36-41, $100-175.

1133. Northern, c. 40, $100-175.

1137. Quandt, c. 34-40, $100-175.

1134. Northern, c. 36-43, $175-250.

1138. Beverwyck, c. 40s-E50s, $50-100.

1135. Ebling, c. L30s-E40s, $100-175.
1136. Ebling, c. L30s-E40s, $100-175.

1139. Yonkers Colonial, c. 34-38, $100-175.

1140. Yonkers Colonial, c. 34-38, $100-175.

North Carolina

1935-0
1945-1
1949-1

1141. Atlantic, c. L30s-40s, $175-250.
1142. Atlantic, c. L30s-40s, $175-250.

Ohio

1935-54
1945-37
1949-31

1143. Matz, c. 40s, $175-250.

1144. Matz, c. 40s, $175-250.

1145. Red Top, c. 50, $175-250.

1146. August Wagner, c. 40s-E50s, $100-175.

1147. Red Top, c. 47-56, $100-175.

1148. Franklin, c. 40s-E50s, $100-175.
1149. Franklin, c. 40s-E50s, $100-175.
1150. Franklin, c. 40s-E50s, $100-175.

1151. Cleveland Home, c. L30s-40s, $100-175.

1152. Ohio, c. 45-48, $175-250.

1153. Bruckmann, c. 36-49, $100-175.
1154. Bruckmann, c. 43, $100-175.

1155. Bruckmann, c. 43, $100-175.
1156. Bruckmann, c. 36-49, $100-175.

1157. Buckeye, c. 50, $100-175.

1158. Buckeye, c. 50, $100-175.
1159. Buckeye, c. 50, $100-175.

1160. Webb, c. 48-52, $175-250.

1161. Burger, c. L30s-40s, $50-100.
1162. Burger, c. L30s-40s, $50-100.

1163. Burger, c. L30s-40s, $50-100.
1164. Burger, c. L30s-40s, $50-100.
1165. Burger, c. L30s-40s, $100-175.

1166. Burger, c. L30s-40s,
$100-175.

1167. Burkhardt, c. 40s-E50s, $50-100.
1168. Burkhardt, c. 40s-E50s, $50-100.
1169. Burkhardt, c. 40s-E50s, $50-100.

1170. Lancaster, c. 34-42,
$100-175.

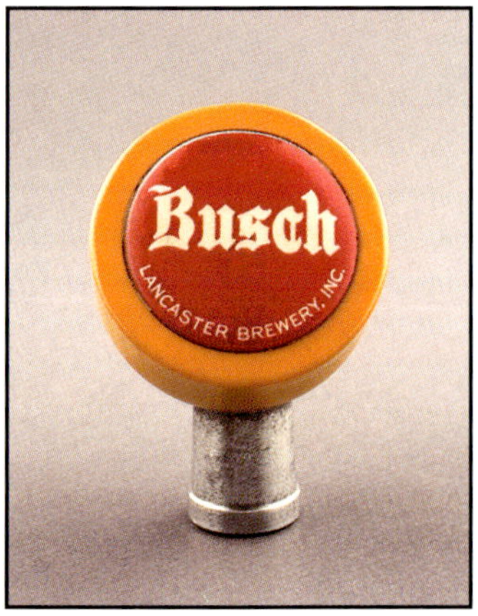

1171. Kings, c. 39-41, $175-250.

1177. Renner, c. 38-48, $100-175.
1178. Renner, c. 40s-E50s, $175-250.
1179. Renner, c. 38-48, $175-250.

1172. Canton, c. 38, $175-250.

1180. Consumers, c. 42-53, $175-250.

1181. Crockery City, c. 36-43, $175-250.

1173. Brew. Co. of Amer., c. 34-45, $100-175.
1174. Brew. Co. of Amer., c. 34-45, $50-100.
1175. Brew. Co. of Amer., c. 34-45, $50-100.

1182. Cleveland-Sandusky, c. 40s-E50s, $175-250.

1176. Brew. Co. of Amer., c. 49, $175-250.

1183. Cleveland-Sandusky, c. 40s-E50s, $175-250.

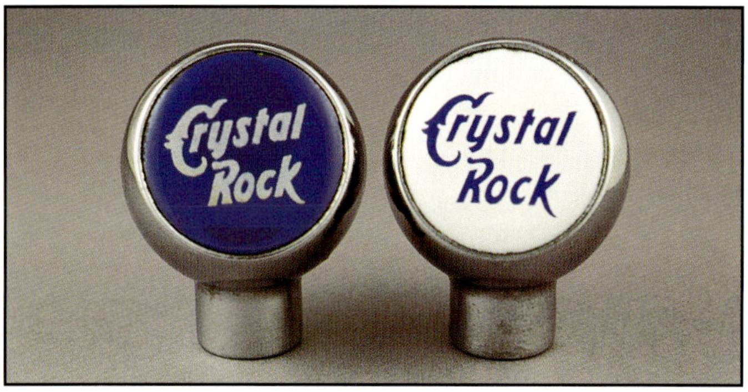

1184. Cleveland-Sandusky, c. 40s-E50s, $100-175.
1185. Cleveland-Sandusky, c. 40s-E50s, $100-175.

1186. Cleveland Home, c. 50-52, $175-250.

1187. Delatron, c. L30s-E40s, $175-250.

1188. Christian Diehl, c. L30s-40s, $100-175.
1189. Christian Diehl, c. 36, $100-175.
1190. Christian Diehl, c. L30s-40s, $100-175.

1191. Eilert, c. 37, $175-250.

1192. Standard, c. 40s-E50s, $100-175.

1193. Clyffside, c. 36-45, $100-175.
1194. Clyffside, c. 36-45, $100-175.

1195. Lancaster, c. 34-42, $250+.

1196. August Wagner, c. 40s-E50s, $100-175.
1197. August Wagner, c. 40s-E50s, $100-175.

1208. Hudepohl, c. 40s-E50s, $175-250.
1209. Hudepohl, c. 50, $100-175.

1201. Hocking Valley, c. L30s-E40s, $175-250.

1198. Cleveland-Sandusky, c. 40s-E50s, $100-175.

1210. Hudepohl, c. 50, $1-25.
1211. Hudepohl, c. 48, $25-50.

1202. Hudepohl, c. 39, $100-175.
1203. Hudepohl, c. 49, $50-100.
1204. Hudepohl, c. 50, $50-100.

1199. Cleveland-Sandusky, c. 40s-E50s, $100-175.

1212. Kings, c. 39-41, $175-250.

1200. Renner, c. 42, $50-100.

1205. Hudepohl, c. 39, $25-50.
1206. Hudepohl, c. 50, $25-50.
1207. Hudepohl, c. 39, $25-50.

1213. Koerber, c. L40s, $175-250.

1214. Koerber, c. L40s,
$100-175.

1215. Leisy, c. 40s-E50s, $50-100.
1216. Leisy, c. 40s-E50s, $50-100.

1217. Leisy, c. 40s-E50s,
$100-175.

1218. Miami Valley, c. 40s-E50s,
$175-250.

1219. Lubeck, c. 36-39,
$100-175.

1220. Milan, c. 40s-E50s,
$175-250.

1221. Youngstown, c. 39-44,
$50-100.

1222. Youngstown, c. 39-44,
$25-50.

1223. Burkhardt, c. 40s-E50s,
$100-175.

1224. Burkhardt, c. 40s-E50s,
$175-250.

1225. Washington, c. 35-52,
$175-250.

1226. New Philadelphia, c. 34-45,
$100-175.

1227. Old Capitol, c. 34-47,
$175-250.

1228. Old Capitol, c. 34-47,
$100-175.

1229. Renner, c. L30s-40s, $175-250.

1230. Renner, c. L30s-40s, $175-250.

1231. Krantz, c. 44-56, $50-100.
1232. Krantz, c. 48, $175-250.
1233. Krantz, c. 44-56, $50-100.

1234. Youngstown, c. 35-37, $175-250.
1235. Renner, c. L30s-40s, $175-250.
1236. Renner, c. L30s-40s, $175-250.

1237. Sunrise, c. 36-38, $175-250.

1238. Freimanns, c. 39, $100-175.

1239. New Philadelphia, c. 35-49, $175-250.

1240. Consumer's, c. 36-43, $175-250.

1241. Renner, c. 40s-E50s, $175-250.

1242. New Philadelphia, c. 36-49, $175-250.

1243. Koerber, c. 34-46, $175-250.

1244. Cleveland-Sandusky, c. 40s-E50s, $175-250.

1245. Cleveland-Sandusky, c. 40s-E50s, $100-175.

1246. Consumer's, c. 36-43, $175-250.

1247. Consumer's, c. 36-43, $175-250.

1248. Consumer's, c. 36-43, $175-250.

1249. Olt Bros., c. 36-41, $175-250.

1253. Pilsener, c. 48, $100-175.
1254. Pilsener, c. 48-52, $50-100.
1255. Pilsener, c. 50, $50-100.

1256. Red Top, c. 39, $100-175.
1257. Red Top, c. 40s-E50s, $100-175.
1258. Red Top, c. 39, $100-175.

1261. Renner, c. L40s, $100-175.

1259. Renner, c. L40s, $100-175.
1260. Renner, c. L40s, $100-175.

1250. Pilsener, c. 48-52, $100-175.
1251. Pilsener, c. 48-52, $50-100.
1252. Pilsener, c. 55, $100-175.

1262. Burger, c. 46, $100-175.

1263. Jackson, c. 34-40, $175-250.

1264. New Philadelphia, c. 36-39, $175-250.

1265. Schoenling, c. E50s, $175-250.

1266. Milan, c. 40s, $175-250.

1267. John Wagner, c. 34-38, $175-250.

1268. Lancaster, c. 37, $50-100.

1269. Renner, c. L30s-40s, $100-175.
1270. Renner, c. L30s-40s, $100-175.

1271. Standard, c. 40s-E50s, $100-175.
1272. Standard, c. 40s-E50s, $100-175.

1273. Star, c. 36-39, $175-250.

1274. Youngstown, c. 34-45, $175-250.

1275. Sunrise, c. 36-38, $175-250.

1276. Tip Top, c. 38-42, $175-250.
1277. Tip Top, c. 38-42, $175-250.

1287. Crockery City, c. 36-43, $175-250.
1288. Webb, c. 37, $175-250.
1289. Crockery City, c. 37, $100-175.

1278. Pilsener, c. 40s, $175-250.

1281. Vienna, c. 38-49, $175-250.

1290. Webb, c. 36-43, $175-250.

1279. Schoenling, c. 46, $175-250.

1282. Forest City, c. 39, $175-250.
1283. Forest City, c. 36-45, $175-250.
1284. Forest City, c. 39, $175-250.

1291. Renner & Weber, c. L30s-40s, $175-250.

1280. Koerber, c. 34-46, $175-250.

1285. Washington, c. L30s-40s, $175-250.
1286. Washington, c. L30s-40s, $175-250.

1292. Akron, c. 36-39, $100-175.

1293. Webb, c. 46-51, $175-250.

1294. Star, c. 39-53, $175-250.

1295. Wunderbrau, c. 51-56, $100-175.

1296. Ohio, c. L40s, $175-250.

Oklahoma

1935-2
1945-2
1949-1

No examples of ball style tap knobs from Oklahoma were found.

Oregon

1935-6
1945-4
1949-2

1297. Blitz Weinhard, c. 48, $50-100.
1298. Blitz Weinhard, c. 47, $100-175.

1299. Blitz Weinhard, c. 37-40, $100-175.
1300. Blitz Weinhard, c. 37-41, $175-250.

1301. Sicks, c. 44-53, $50-100.

1302. Sicks, c. 44-53, $50-100.

1303. Salem, c. 37, $100-175.

Pennsylvania

1935-108
1945-62
1949-55

1304. Lebanon Valley, c. L30s-40s, $50-100.

1305. Mt. Carmel, c. 40-49, $50-100.

1306. Mt. Carbon, c. 38, $25-50.

1307. Altoona, c. 40-45, $25-50.

1308. Chartiers Valley, c. 36-41, $250+.

1309. Chartiers Valley, c. 36-41, $100-175.

1310. Latrobe, c. L30s, $250+.

1311. Bartels, c. 47, $25-50.
1312. Bartels, c. 47, $25-50.

1313. Bartels, c. 47, $25-50.

1314. Mt. Carbon, c. 40s, $25-50.
1315. Mt. Carbon, c. 40s, $25-50.

1316. Mt. Carbon, c. 40s, $25-50.

1317. Mt. Carbon, c. 40s, $25-50.
1318. Mt. Carbon, c. 40s, $25-50.

1319. Old Reading, c. 40s, $25-50.

1320. John F. Betz, c. 35, $100-175.

1321. Mt. Carmel, c. 40-49, $50-100.

1322. Pittsburgh, c. 37-46, $100-175.

1323. Jenner Springs, c. 36-38, $175-250.

1324. Moose, c. L30s-40s, $100-175.

1325. Moose, c. L30s-40s, $100-175.

1326. Moose, c. L30s-40s, $100-175.

1327. Boyertown, c. L30s-40s, $100-175.

1328. Bushkill, c. 36-41, $100-175.

1329. Bushkill, c. 37, $100-175.
1330. Bushkill, c. 37, $100-175.

1331. Tube City, c. 38-46, $100-175.

1332. Cambria, c. 34-37, $175-250.

1333. Chartiers Valley, c. 34-41, $175-250.
1334. Chartiers Valley, c. 38, $50-100.
1335. Chartiers Valley, c. 38, $50-100.

1336. Eagle, c. 34-45, $100-175.

1337. Chester, c. 40, $175-250.

1338. Chester, c. 40, $100-175.
1339. Chester, c. 40, $100-175.
1340. Chester, c. 40, $100-175.

1341. Lockport, c. 36-39, $175-250.

1342. Helbs Keystone, c. 41-49, $100-175.

1343. Columbia, c. 49, $25-50.
1344. Columbia, c. 49, $50-100.
1345. Columbia, c. 49, $50-100.

1346. Liebert & Obert, c. L30s-E40s, $50-100.
1347. Liebert & Obert, c. 41, $50-100.
1348. Liebert & Obert, c. L30s-E40s, $25-50.

1355. Daeufer-Lieberman, c. 36-40, $25-50.
1356. Daeufer-Lieberman, c. 36-40, $25-50.

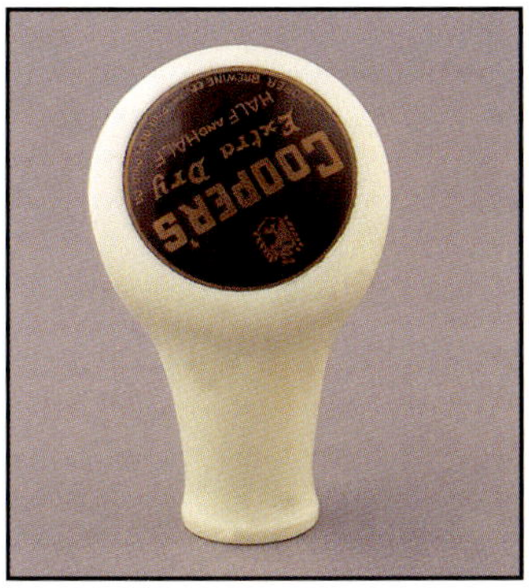

1349. Liebert & Obert, c. L30s-E40s, $50-100.

1357. Deppen, c. 36-37, $100-175.
1358. Deppen, c. 36-37, $100-175.

1350. Cooper, c. L30s-E40s, $50-100.
1351. Cooper, c. 40, $50-100.
1352. Liebert & Obert, c. L30s-E40s, $50-100.

1359. Beth Uhl, c. 40-41, $100-175.

1360. Mt. Carbon, c. 34-38, $25-50.

1353. Cooper, c. 46-48, $50-100.

1354. Standard, c. 40, $50-100.

1361. Du Bois, c. 40s-E50s, $50-100.
1362. Du Bois, c. 40s-E50s, $50-100.
1363. Du Bois, c. 40s-E50s, $50-100.

1364. Duquesne, c. 40s-E50s, $1-25.
1365. Duquesne, c. L30s-40s, $25-50.

1366. Duquesne, c. L30s-40s, $25-50.
1367. Duquesne, c. L30s-40s, $25-50.
1368. Duquesne, c. L30s-40s, $25-50.

1369. Duquesne, c. E50s, $25-50.
1370. Duquesne, c. L30s-40s, $25-50.
1371. Duquesne, c. 34-40, $175-250.

1372. Eberhardt & Ober, c. 40, $25-50.
1373. Eberhardt & Ober, c. 40, $25-50.
1374. Eberhardt & Ober, c. 40, $25-50.

1375. Eberhardt & Ober, c. 35-42, $25-50.
1376. Eberhardt & Ober, c. 35-42, $50-100.

1377. Pittston, c. 34-42, $100-175.

1378. Deppen, c. 36-37, $100-175.

1379. Eberhardt & Ober, c. 39, $25-50.

1380. Eberhardt & Ober,
c. 40, $25-50 (f).

1381. Otto Erlanger, c. L30s-40s, $50-100.
1382. Otto Erlanger, c. L30s-40s, $50-100.

1383. Otto Erlanger,
c. L30s-40s, $25-50.

1384. Otto Erlanger, c. 42-50, $25-50.
1385. Esslingers, c. 41, $100-175.
1386. Esslingers, c. 41, $100-175.

1387. Esslingers, c. 41, $50-100.
1388. Esslingers, c. 41, $50-100.
1389. Esslingers, c. 41, $50-100.

1390. Esslingers, c. 41, $100-175.
1391. Esslingers, c. 41, $100-175.

1392. Esslingers, c. 34-77,
$25-50.

1393. Fuhrmann & Schmidt, c. 47, $25-50.
1394. Fuhrmann & Schmidt, c. 47, $25-50.

1395. Fuhrmann & Schmidt, c. 47, $25-50.
1396. Fuhrmann & Schmidt, c. 47, $25-50.

1403. Flock, c. 45, $100-175.

1397. Fell, c. L30s-40s, $100-175.
1398. Fell, c. L30s-40s, $100-175.

1404. West Masontown,
c. 34-39, $175-250.

1399. Flock, c. 45, $50-100.
1400. Flock, c. 45, $50-100.
1401. Flock, c. 45, $50-100.

1405. Fort Pitt, c. 40s, $25-50.
1406. Fort Pitt, c. 40s, $25-50 (f).

1402. Flock, c. 45, $50-100.

1407. Fort Pitt, c. 40s, $50-100.

1408. Fort Pitt, c. 40s, $1-25.

1409. Franklin, c. 40s-E50s, $25-50.
1410. Franklin, c. 40s-E50s, $50-100.
1411. Franklin, c. 40s-E50s, $25-50.

1412. Freeland, c. 36-40, $50-100.

1416. Goenner, c. L30s-40s, $250+.

1413. Freeland, c. 36-40, $50-100.

1417. Chartiers Valley, c. 36-41, $175-250.

1414. Mauch Chunk, c. 36-41, $175-250.
1415. Mauch Chunk, c. 36-41, $100-175.

1418. Lockport, c. 41, $50-100.
1419. Lockport, c. 48, $100-175.

1420. Lion, c. 34-40, $25-50.
1421. Lion, c. L30s-40s, $50-100.

1422. Lion, c. 34-40, $25-50.
1423. Lion, c. 34-40, $50-100.

1424. Lion, c. 34-40, $50-100.

1425. Lion, c. 34-40, $100-175.

1426. Pittston, c. 34-42,
$100-175.

1427. Pittston, c. 34-42,
$100-175.

1428. Goenner, c. L30s-40s, $100-175.
1429. Goenner, c. L30s-40s, $100-175.
1430. Goenner, c. L30s-40s, $100-175.

1431. Goenner, c. L30s-40s,
$100-175.

1432. Ferwood, c. 36-41, $100-175.
1433. Ferwood, c. 37, $100-175.

1434. Robt. H. Graupner, c. L30s-40s, $50-100.
1435. Robt. H. Graupner, c. 40s-E50s, $100-175.

1436. Robt. H. Graupner, c. L30s-40s, $100-175.
1437. Robt. H. Graupner, c. L30s-40s, $100-175.

1438. Robt. H. Graupner, c. L30s-40s, $50-100.
1439. Robt. H. Graupner, c. L40s, $50-100.
1440. Robt. H. Graupner, c. L40s, $50-100.

1441. Robt. H. Graupner, c. L30s-40s, $25-50.
1442. Robt. H. Graupner, c. L30s-40s, $25-50.

1443. Wm. Gretz, c. 50, $25-50.
1444. Wm. Gretz, c. 50, $1-25.
1445. Wm. Gretz, c. 50, $25-50.

1446. Wm. Gretz, c. 40s-E50s, $100-175.
1447. Wm. Gretz, c. 40s-E50s, $100-175.

1454. Helbs Keystone, c. 34-36, $175-250.

1456. Hofbrau, c. 40s-E50s, $50-100.

1448. Wm. Gretz, c. 40s-E50s, $50-100.

1450. Haefner, c. 34-40, $100-175.

1455. Homestead, c. 35-53, $100-175.

1449. Class & Nachod, c. 36, $100-175.

1451. Pilsener, c. 40s-E50s, $100-175.
1452. Pilsener, c. 40s-E50s, $50-100.
1453. Pilsener, c. 40s-E50s, $100-175.

1457. Jos. Hohenadel, c. L30s-40s, $25-50.
1458. Jos. Hohenadel, c. L30s-40s, $1-25.

1469. Jacob Hornung, c. L30s-40s, $50-100.
1470. Jacob Hornung, c. L30s-40s, $50-100.
1471. Jacob Hornung, c. L30s-40s, $50-100.

1459. Jos. Hohenadel, c. 37,
$25-50.

1460. Jos. Hohenadel, c. 40,
$50-100.

1461. Homestead, c. 34-45,
$50-100.

1462. Homestead Ice, c. L30s-E40s, $100-175.
1463. Homestead Ice, c. L30s-E40s, $100-175.

1464. Horlacher, c. L30s-40s, $100-175.
1465. Horlacher, c. L30s-40s, $50-100.
1466. Horlacher, c. L30s-40s, $100-175.

1467. Horlacher, c. L30s-40s,
$100-175.

1468. Horlacher, c. L30s-40s,
$100-175.

1472. Jacob Hornung, c. 48, $50-100.
1473. Jacob Hornung, c. L30s-40s, $100-175.
1474. Jacob Hornung, c. 48, $50-100.

1475. Jacob Hornung, c. L30s-40s, $50-100.
1476. Jacob Hornung, c. L30s-40s, $50-100.

1477. John Hohenadel, c. L30s-40s, $175-250.

1478. Pittsburgh, c. 30s, $100-175.
1479. Pittsburgh, c. L30s, $100-175.

1480. Pittsburgh, c. L30s, $50-100.
1481. Pittsburgh, c. L30s, $100-175.
1482. Pittsburgh, c. L30s, $50-100.

1483. Robt. H. Graupner, c. L40s, $100-175.

1484. Robt. H. Graupner, c. L40s, $100-175.

1485. Chas D. Kaier, c. 41, $1-25.
1486. Chas D. Kaier, c. 41, $25-50.

1487. Chas D. Kaier, c. 41, $25-50.
1488. Chas D. Kaier, c. 41, $25-50.
1489. Chas D. Kaier, c. 41, $25-50.

1490. Chas D. Kaier, c. 41, $50-100.
1491. Chas D. Kaier, c. 41, $25-50.
1492. Chas D. Kaier, c. 41, $25-50.

1493. Chas D. Kaier, c. 41, $25-50.

1494. Chas D. Kaier, c. 41, $25-50.

1495. Keystone, c. 35, $100-175.
1496. Keystone, c. 35, $100-175.

1497. Erie, c. 48, $25-50.

1498. Kuebler, c. L30s-40s, $50-100.
1499. Kuebler, c. L30s-40s, $50-100.
1500. Kuebler, c. 41, $50-100.

1501. Kuebler, c. L30s-40s, $25-50.

1502. Kuebler, c. L30s-40s, $100-175.
1503. Kuebler, c. L30s-40s, $100-175.

1504. Kuebler, c. L30s-40s, $50-100.
1505. Kuebler, c. L30s-40s, $50-100.
1506. Kuebler, c. L30s-40s, $100-175.

1514. Lebanon, c. L30s-40s, $50-100.
1515. Lebanon, c. L30s-40s, $50-100.
1516. Lebanon, c. L30s-40s, $50-100.

1517. Lebanon, c. L30s-40s, $50-100.

1507. Lackawanna, c. 36-43, $100-175.

1509. Latrobe, c. 34-40, $175-250.
1510. Latrobe, c. 34-40, $175-250.
1511. Latrobe, c. 34-40, $175-250.

1518. Liebert & Obert, c. L30s-E40s, $100-175.

1508. Latrobe, c. 34-40, $175-250.

1512. Lebanon, c. L30s-40s, $100-175.
1513. Lebanon, c. L30s-40s, $50-100.

1519. Liebert & Obert, c. L30s-E40s, $50-100.

1520. Wacker, c. L30s-40s, $100-175.

1524. Philadelphia, c. L30s-E40s, $100-175.
1525. Philadelphia, c. L30s-E40s, $50-100.
1526. Philadelphia, c. L30s-40s, $50-100.

1521. Lockport, c. 36-39, $250+.

1527. Philadelphia, c. L30s-E40s, $50-100.

1531. Homestead, c. 49-53, $175-250.

1522. Jacob Hornung, c. 34-40, $100-175.

1528. Mt. Carmel, c. 39-51, $100-175.

1532. Mt. Carbon, c. L30s-40s, $50-100.
1533. Mt. Carbon, c. L30s-40s, $50-100.

1523. Liebert & Obert, c. L30s-E40s, $100-175.

1529. Moose, c. 36-49, $100-175.
1530. Moose, c. 36-49, $100-175.

1534. Mt. Carbon, c. 35-43, $50-100.
1535. Mt. Carbon, c. 35-43, $25-50.
1536. Mt. Carbon, c. 35-43, $25-50.

1537. Mt. Carmel, c. 40-49, $100-175.

1538. Sprenger, c. L30s-40s, $100-175.

1539. Cooper, c. 46-48, $50-100.

1540. Cooper, c. 46-48, $100-175.

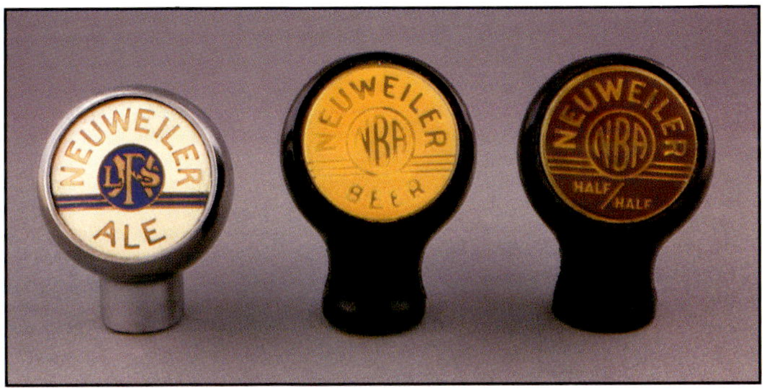

1541. Louis F. Neuweiler, c. 40s-E50s, $50-100.
1542. Louis F. Neuweiler, c. 40s-E50s, $50-100.
1543. Louis F. Neuweiler, c. 53-57, $50-100.

1544. Louis F. Neuweiler, c. 40s-E50s, $50-100.
1545. Louis F. Neuweiler, c. 40s-E50s, $50-100.

1546. Louis F. Neuweiler, c. 40s-E50s, $50-100.
1547. Louis F. Neuweiler, c. L30s-40s, $50-100.
1548. Louis F. Neuweiler, c. L30s-40s, $50-100.

1556. Louis F. Neuweiler, c. 50-54, $50-100.

1549. Louis F. Neuweiler, c. L30s-40s, $100-175.

1557. Brackenridge, c. 36-45, $100-175.

1550. Louis F. Neuweiler, c. 40s-E50s, $25-50.
1551. Louis F. Neuweiler, c. L30s-40s, $25-50.
1552. Louis F. Neuweiler, c. L30s-40s, $25-50.

1558. Brackenridge, c. 36-45, $25-50 (f).

1553. Louis F. Neuweiler, c. 40s-E50s, $25-50.

1554. Goenner, c. L30s-40s, $50-100.
1555. Goenner, c. L30s-40s, $50-100.

1559. Wacker, c. 46-53, $100-175.

1564. Eagle, c. 40s, $50-100.
1565. Eagle, c. 40s, $50-100.

1560. Mt. Carbon, c. 40s, $25-50 (f).

1566. Lockport, c. 35-40, $100-175.

1568. Mt. Carbon, c. 47-51, $100-175.
1569. Mt. Carbon, c. 47-51, $100-175.

1561. Erie, c. 48, $100-175.

1567. Mt. Carbon, c. 47-51, $100-175.

1570. Northampton, c. L30s-40s, $50-100.

1572. Washington, c. 34-40, $175-250.

1562. Eagle, c. 40s, $100-175.
1563. Eagle, c. 40s, $100-175.

1571. Northampton, c. L30s-40s, $50-100.

1573. Lebanon Valley, c. L30s-40s, $50-100.
1574. Haefner, c. 34-40, $25-50.
1575. Mt. Carmel, c. 42-49, $50-100.

1576. Mt. Carbon, c. 42-49,
$100-175.

1577. Mt. Carbon, c. 42-49, $50-100.
1578. Lion, c. 37-45, $25-50.

1579. Lion, c. 37-45, $25-50.
1580. Ashland, c. 35-38, $50-100.
1581. Haefner, c. 34-40, $50-100.

1582. Old Indian, c. 36-38,
$175-250.

1583. Pittsburgh, c. 35-39,
$175-250.

1584. Pittston, c. 34-42,
$175-250.

1585. National, c. 38-39,
$100-175.

1586. Old Reading, c. 40s-E50s, $50-100.
1587. Old Reading, c. 40s-E50s, $50-100.
1588. Old Reading, c. 40s-E50s, $50-100.

1597. Fort Pitt, c. 48, $100-175.

1589. Old Reading, c. 40s-E50s, $50-100.
1590. Old Reading, c. 40s-E50s, $25-50.
1591. Old Reading, c. 40s-E50s, $25-50.

1598. Philadelphia, c. 36-44, $50-100.
1599. Philadelphia, c. 36-44, $50-100.
1600. Philadelphia, c. 36-44, $50-100.

1592. Old Reading, c. 40s-E50s, $50-100.
1593. Old Reading, c. 40s-E50s, $100-175.

1601. Philadelphia, c. 36-44, $25-50.

1602. Philadelphia, c. 39, $100-175.

1594. Old Reliable, c. 38-41, $250+.

1595. Fort Pitt, c. 48, $25-50.
1596. Fort Pitt, c. 48, $50-100.

1603. Philadelphia, c. 39, $50-100.
1604. Philadelphia, c. 39, $50-100.
1605. Philadelphia, c. 39, $50-100.

1606. Philadelphia, c. 35-49, $50-100.

1607. Philadelphia, c. 40s, $50-100.
1608. Philadelphia, c. 40s, $25-50.
1609. Philadelphia, c. 40-47, $50-100.

1610. Old Lancaster, c. 36-38, $100-175.

1611. Henry F. Ortlieb, c. 39, $25-50.
1612. Henry F. Ortlieb, c. 39, $25-50.
1613. Henry F. Ortlieb, c. 40s, $25-50.

1614. Henry F. Ortlieb, c. 40s, $50-100.

1615. Penn Star, c. 46-59, $175-250.

1616. Moose, c. 37, $100-175.
1617. Moose, c. 40, $100-175.

1618. Howell & King, c. 34-39, $100-175.

1619. Otto Erlanger, c. 38-45, $175-250.

1620. Flock, c. 40s-E50s, $175-250.

1621. Altoona, c. 41, $50-100.

1622. Sprenger, c. L30s-40s, $25-50.

1623. Sprenger, c. L30s-40s, $25-50.

1624. Du Bois, c. 40s-E50s, $175-250.

1625. Altoona, c. 40s, $50-100.

1626. Poth, c. 37-41, $100-175.

1627. Poth, c. 37-41, $100-175.

1628. Poth, c. 37-41, $100-175.

1629. Adam Scheidt, c. 40s-E50s, $25-50.
1630. Adam Scheidt, c. 40s-E50s, $25-50.

1631. Adam Scheidt, c. 40s-E50s, $25-50.

1632. Adam Scheidt, c. 47, $25-50.
1633. Adam Scheidt, c. 47, $25-50.

1634. Adam Scheidt, c. 40s-E50s, $25-50.

1635. Adam Scheidt, c. 44-56, $25-50.

1636. Penn Star, c. 36-38, $100-175.

1637. Penn Star, c. 36-38, $100-175.

1638. Latrobe, c. 50, $50-100.

1639. General Braddock, c. 36-37, $175-250.

1640. Widman, c. 35-38, $100-175.

1641. Union, c. 38-47, $100-175.

1642. Haefner, c. 34-40, $50-100.

1643. Schiller, c. 40-41, $100-175.

1644. C. Schmidt, c. L30s, $100-175.

1645. Ashland, c. 35-38, $100-175.

1646. Seitz, c. 36-39, $50-100.

1647. Chester, c. 42, $50-100.
1648. Chester, c. 42, $50-100.

1649. Graupner's, c. 40s-E50s, $50-100.

1650. Duquesne, c. L30s-40s, $100-175.

1651. Duquesne, c. L30s-40s, $50-100.

1652. South Fork, c. 36-40, $175-250.

1653. South Fork, c. 36-40, $175-250.

1654. Pittsburgh, c. L30s, $175-250.

1655. Sprenger, c. L30s-40s, $100-175.

1656. St. Mary's, c. 36-40, $250+.

1657. Stag, c. 34, $250+.

1658. Standard, c. 40s, $50-100.
1659. Standard, c. 40s, $50-100.

1660. Standard, c. L30s-E40s, $50-100.

1661. Standard, c. L30s-E40s, $100-175.

1662. Stegmaier, c. 40s-E50s, $50-100.
1663. Stegmaier, c. 40s-E50s, $25-50.
1664. Stegmaier, c. 46, $25-50.

1665. Stegmaier, c. 53, $25-50.
1666. Stegmaier, c. 53, $25-50.
1667. Stegmaier, c. 53, $25-50.

1668. Stegmaier, c. 53, $50-100.
1669. Stegmaier, c. E50s, $25-50 (f).
1670. Stegmaier, c. 50, $50-100.

1671. Stegmaier, c. 46, $25-50.
1672. Stegmaier, c. 53, $25-50.
1673. Stegmaier, c. 46, $25-50.

1674. Fort Pitt, c. 34-43, $175-250.
1675. Victor, c. 34-43, $175-250.

1676. Victor, c. 34-43, $175-250.

1677. Jones, c. L30s, $100-175.
1678. Jones, c. L30s, $100-175.

1679. Jones, c. L30s, $100-175.
1680. Jones, c. L30s, $175-250.
1681. Jones, c. L30s, $250+.

1682. Jones, c. L30s, $50-100.

1683. Straub, c. L30s, $100-175.
1684. Straub, c. L30s, $100-175.

1685. Straub, c. L30s, $100-175.

1687. Sunbury, c. 35-37, $100-175.

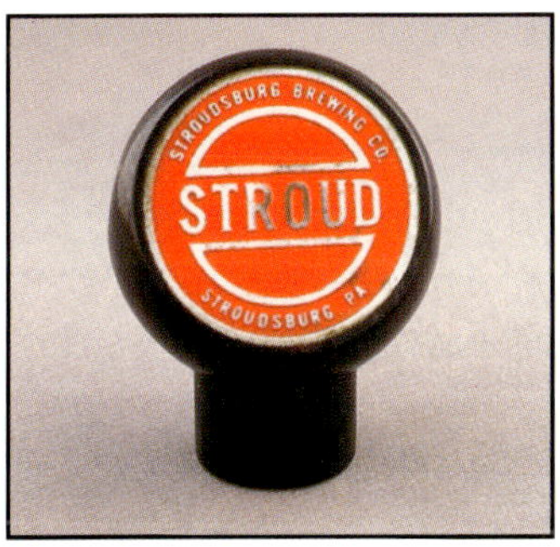

1686. Stroudsburg, c. 35-37, $100-175.

1688. Barbey's, c. 40s-E50s, $50-100.
1689. Barbey's, c. 40s-E50s, $50-100.

1690. Barbey's, c. 40s-E50s, $100-175.
1691. Barbey's, c. 40s-E50s, $50-100.
1692. Barbey's, c. 40s-E50s, $50-100.

1693. Barbey's, c. 42, $50-100.
1694. Barbey's, c. 40s-E50s, $50-100.
1695. Barbey's, c. 42, $50-100.

1696. South Bethlehem, c. 47, $50-100.
1697. South Bethlehem, c. 47, $50-100.
1698. South Bethlehem, c. 47, $50-100.

1699. Beth Uhl, c. 36-41, $100-175.
1700. Beth Uhl, c. 36-41, $100-175.
1701. Beth Uhl, c. 36-41, $100-175.

1702. Beth Uhl, c. 36-41, $175-250.

1703. Pittsburgh, c. L30s, $50-100.
1704. Pittsburgh, c. L30s, $50-100.
1705. Pittsburgh, c. L30s, $100-175.

1706. Pittsburgh, c. L30s, $25-50 (f).
1707. Pittsburgh, c. L30s, $50-100.

1708. Standard, c. 40s, $50-100.
1709. Standard, c. 40s, $50-100.

1710. Northampton, c. 39, $50-100.
1711. Northampton, c. 39, $50-100.
1712. Northampton, c. 39, $50-100.

1713. Northampton, c. 39, $100-175.
1714. Northampton, c. 40s-E50s, $25-50 (f).
1715. Northampton, c. 40s-E50s, $100-175.

1716. Tube City, c. L30s-40s, $100-175.
1717. Tube City, c. L30s-40s, $100-175.

1718. Robt. H. Graupner, c. 38-46, $100-175.

1719. Beth Uhl, c. 36-41, $175-250.

1720. Union, c. 36-43, $175-250.
1721. Union, c. 37, $100-175.

1722. Union, c. 36-43, $175-250.

1723. Adam Scheidt, c. 40s-E50s, $25-50.
1724. Adam Scheidt, c. 42, $25-50.
1725. Adam Scheidt, c. 40s-E50s, $25-50.

1726. Adam Scheidt, c. 37-59, $25-50.
1727. Adam Scheidt, c. 42, $25-50.
1728. Adam Scheidt, c. 37-59, $25-50.

1729. Adam Scheidt, c. 40s-E50s, $25-50.

1731. Wacker, c. 38-54, $100-175.

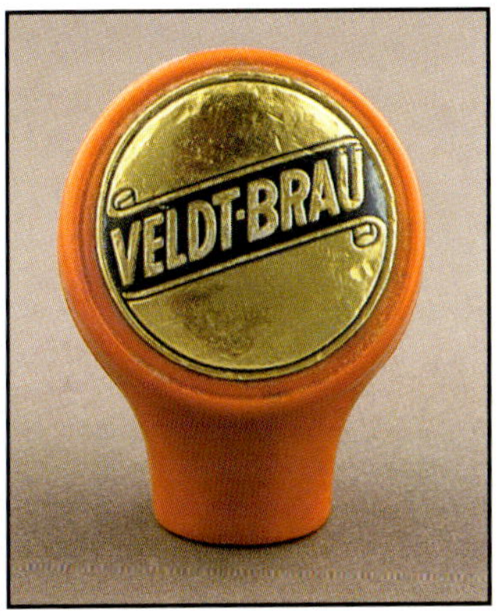

1730. Chester, c. 40s, $25-50 (f).

1732. Washington, c. 34-40, $175-250.

1733. Washington, c. 34-40, $100-175.
1734. Washington, c. 38, $175-250.

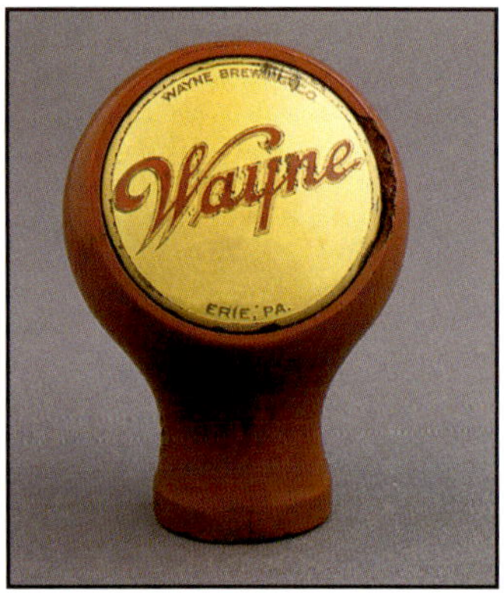

1735. Wayne, c. L30s-40s, $50-100.

1736. Wayne, c. L30s-40s, $50-100.

1737. Weisbrod & Hess, c. 36-37, $100-175.

1738. Weisbrod & Hess, c. 36-37, $100-175.

1739. Wentzler, c. 37, $100-175.

1740. Northampton, c. L30s-40s, $100-175.
1741. Northampton, c. 41, $50-100.
1742. Northampton, c. L30s-40s, $100-175.

1743. Northampton, c. L30s-40s, $100-175.
1744. Northampton, c. 41, $50-100.
1745. Northampton, c. L30s-40s, $100-175.

1746. Northampton, c. L30s-40s, $100-175.

1747. Widman, c. 34-38, $100-175.

1748. Woerner, c. 35-38, $100-175.

1749. John Jacob Wolf, c. 36, $100-175.

1750. Adam Scheidt, c. 40s-E50s, $100-175.

1751. Champ, c. 46-48, $50-100.
1752. Champ, c. 46-48, $50-100.
1753. Champ, c. 46-48, $50-100.

1754. Union, c. 34-40, $175-250.

1755. Yough, c. 37, $175-250.

1756. Yough, c. L30s-40s, $100-175.

1757. D. G. Yuengling, c. 53, $25-50.
1758. D. G. Yuengling, c. 53, $25-50.
1759. D. G. Yuengling, c. 53, $25-50.

1760. D. G. Yuengling, c. 53, $25-50.
1761. D. G. Yuengling, c. 53, $25-50.

Rhode Island

1935-6
1945-2
1949-2

1762. Narragansett, c. 40s, $100-175.

1770. Narragansett, c. 40s-E50s, $50-100.
1771. Narragansett, c. 40s-E50s, $50-100.
1772. Narragansett, c. 40s-E50s, $50-100.

1763. James Hanley, c. E50s, $50-100.
1764. James Hanley, c. E50s, $50-100.
1765. James Hanley, c. E50s, $100-175.

1773. Narragansett, c. 40s-E50s, $50-100.
1774. Narragansett, c. 40s-E50s, $50-100.
1775. Narragansett, c. 40s-E50s, $50-100.

1766. James Hanley, c. E50s, $100-175.

1768. James Hanley, c. E50s, $50-100.

1767. James Hanley, c. E50s, $100-175.

1769. Hollen, c. 36-38, $100-175.

1776. Narragansett, c. 40s-E50s, $50-100.
1777. Narragansett, c. 40s-E50s, $100-175.
1778. Narragansett, c. 40s-E50s, $50-100.

1779. Narragansett, c. 40s-E50s, $100-175.

1780. Narragansett, c. 40s-E50s, $25-50.
1781. Narragansett, c. 40s-E50s, $25-50.

1782. James Hanley, c. 47, $50-100.

1783. Roger Williams, c. 35-39, $175-250.

South Dakota

1935-1
1945-0
1949-0

No examples of ball style tap knobs from South Dakota were found.

Tennessee

1935-3
1945-2
1949-2

1784. Wm. Gerst, c. L30s-40s, $250+.

Texas

1935-10
1945-7
1949-7

1785. Harry Mitchell, c. 36-39, $175-250.

1786. Lone Star, c. 46, $175-250.

1787. San Antonio, c. L30s-40s, $175-250.

1788. Spoetzl, c. 36-39, $175-250.

1789. Galveston-Houston, c. 40s-E50s, $100-175.

Utah

1935-2
1945-2
1949-2

1790. Becker, c. 36, $250+.

1791. Fisher, c. 40s-E50s, $175-250.

Virginia

1935-2
1945-4
1949-4

1792. Southern, c. 35-42, $175-250.

1793. Home, c. L30s-40s, $100-175.

Washington

1935-18
1945-11
1949-10

1794. Columbia, c. 36-49, $50-100.
1795. Columbia, c. 38, $50-100.

1796. Bohemian, c. 40s, $100-175.

1797. Columbia, c. 40, $100-175.

1798. Silver Springs, c. 47-50, $175-250.

1799. Spokane, c. 38, $100-175.

1800. Spokane, c. 37-44, $175-250.

1801. Spokane, c. 36-37, $100-175.

1802. Spokane, c. 36-37, $175-250.

1803. Mutual, c. 37, $100-175.

1804. Golden Age, c. 39, $100-175.
1805. Golden Age, c. L30s-E40s, $100-175.

1806. Hemrich, c. 36, $100-175.

1807. Hennrich, c. 34-39, $175-250.

1808. United Union, c. 35-39, $175-250.

1809. United Union, c. 36, $175-250.

1810. Silver Springs, c. E50s, $175-250.

1811. Mutual, c. 34-43, $175-250.

1812. Olympia, c. 42, $100-175.

1813. Olympia, c. 42, $50-100.

1814. Pioneer, c. 36-44, $175-250.
1815. Pioneer, c. 36-44, $100-175.

1816. Pioneer, c. 44-48,
$100-175.

1817. Sicks Seattle, c. 44-56, $50-100.
1818. Sicks Seattle, c. 44-56, $100-175.

1819. Rheinlander, c. 42-45, $50-100.
1820. Seattle, c. 35-44, $100-175.

1821. Yakima Valley, c. 38,
$100-175.

1822. Seattle, c. 43-56, $50-100.
1823. Seattle, c. 43-56, $50-100.
1824. Seattle, c. 43-56, $50-100.

1825. Sick Century, c. 38-41, $50-100.

1826. Star, c. 35-39, $175-250.

1827. United Union, c. 36-45, $175-250.

1828. Horluck, c. 36-39, $175-250.

West Virginia

1935-4
1945-1
1949-1

1829. Fesenmeier, c. 36-49, $175-250.

Wisconsin

1935-86
1945-60
1949-52

1830. Denmark, c. L30s-E40s, $175-250.

1831. Wausau, c. 50s, $100-175.
1832. Wausau, c. 50s, $100-175.
1833. Wausau, c. 50s, $100-175.

1834. Geo. Walter, c. 47, $50-100.

1835. Green Bay, c. E50s, $250+.

1839. Whitewater, c. 37, $100-175.
1840. Whitewater, c. 39, $175-250.

1836. Bloomer, c. L30s-E40s, $175-250.

1841. Kewaunee, c. 36-39, $175-250.

1846. Binzel, c. 36-39, $175-250.

1837. Pabst, c. 49, $50-100.

1842. Berlin, c. L40s, $175-250.

1847. Blatz, c. 50, $50-100.
1848. Blatz, c. 50, $50-100.
1849. Blatz, c. 49, $100-175.

1838. Arcadia, c. 34-40, $250+.

1843. Berlin, c. L40s, $100-175.
1844. Berlin, c. L40s, $50-100.
1845. Berlin, c. 36, $100-175.

1850. Blatz, c. 40s-E50s, $100-175.
1851. Blatz, c. 40s-E50s, $100-175.

1852. Blatz, c. 45, $50-100.
1853. Blatz, c. 48, $50-100.
1854. Blatz, c. 45, $100-175.

1855. Blatz, c. 45, $50-100.
1856. Blatz, c. 49, $50-100.
1857. Blatz, c. 45, $50-100.

1858. Blatz, c. 45, $50-100.
1859. Blatz, c. 45, $50-100.

1860. Bleser, c. 36-39, $175-250.

1861. Two Rivers, c. 36,
$175-250.

1862. Two Rivers, c. 36,
$175-250.

1863. Independent Milwaukee, c. 43, $100-175.
1864. Independent Milwaukee, c. 40s-E50s, $100-175.
1865. Independent Milwaukee, c. 40s-E50s, $50-100.

1866. Independent Milwaukee, c. 40s-E50s, $50-100.
1867. Independent Milwaukee, c. 40s-E50s, $50-100.

1874. Harold C. Johnson, c. 51, $100-175.

1868. Rice Lake, c. 40s-E50s, $100-175.
1869. Rice Lake, c. 40s-E50s, $100-175.

1875. Oshkosh, c. 48, $50-100.
1876. Oshkosh, c. 41, $100-175.
1877. Oshkosh, c. 40-46, $100-175.

1870. Burlington, c. 35-39, $175-250.

1872. Calumet, c. 34-37, $175-250.

1878. Capitol, c. L30s-E40s, $175-250.

1880. Whitewater, c. 36-43, $175-250.

1871. Burlington, c. 35-39, $175-250.

1873. Capitol, c. L30s-E40s, $175-250.

1879. Wisconsin Coop, c. 37-42, $175-250.

1881. Bleser, c. 37-42, $175-250.

1882. Carl Ebner, c. L30s-E40s, $100-175.

1883. Effinger, c. 34-37, $100-175.

1884. Effinger, c. 34-37, $175-250.

1885. Bechauds, c. 36-41, $175-250.

1886. Eulberg, c. L30s-40s, $100-175.

1887. Fauerbach, c. 40s-E50s, $175-250.

1888. Fauerbach, c. 40s-E50s, $175-250.

1889. Fauerbach, c. L40s, $100-175.

1890. Fox Valley, c. 34-41, $175-250.

1891. Fountain, c. 40s-E50s, $175-250.

1892. Fox Head, c. 41, $100-175.
1893. Fox Head, c. 41, $100-175.
1894. Fox Head, c. 35-47, $100-175.

1895. Fox Lake, c. 34-37, $175-250.

1896. Fox Valley, c. 34-41, $100-175.

1897. Walter Bros., c. 50, $100-175.
1898. Walter Bros., c. 34-57, $100-175.

1899. Walter Bros., c. 49,
$100-175.

1900. A. Gettelmann, c. 50, $100-175.
1901. A. Gettelmann, c. 40s-E50s, $50-100.

1906. Bleser, c. 36-39, $250+.

1907. Walter Bros., c. 34-39,
$100-175.

1908. Walter Bros., c. L30s-40s, $100-175.
1909. Walter Bros., c. L30s-40s, $100-175.

1902. Gettelman, c. 40s-E50s,
$50-100.

1903. A. Gettelmann, c. 48, $100-175.
1904. A. Gettelmann, c. 48, $50-100.
1905. A. Gettelmann, c. 50, $100-175.

1910. Mathie Ruder, c. 39, $100-175.

1911. Two Rivers, c. L30s-E40s, $175-250.

1912. Blumer, c. 47, $250+.

1913. Blumer, c. 36-43, $175-250.

1914. Blumer, c. 36-43, $175-250.

1915. Blumer, c. 38-47, $175-250.

1916. Blumer, c. 38-47, $175-250.

1917. Semrad-Pusch, c. 33-42, $175-250.

1918. Hillsboro, c. 37-43, $175-250.
1919. Louis Ziegler, c. 44-49, $175-250.

1920. Hochgreve, c. 36-49, $175-250.
1921. Hochgreve, c. 36-49, $100-175.

1922. Jos. Huber, c. 47-55, $175-250.

1923. Independent Milwaukee, c. 34-37, $100-175.

1924. Perplies, c. L30s-E40s, $175-250.

1925. Wm. G. Jung, c. 40s, $100-175.
1926. Wm. G. Jung, c. 40s, $100-175.

1927. Wm. G. Jung, c. 40s, $100-175.
1928. Wm. G. Jung, c. 40s, $100-175.

1929. Wm. G. Jung, c. 40s, $100-175.

1930. Kingsbury, c. 46, $100-175.
1931. Kingsbury, c. 46, $50-100.
1932. Kingsbury, c. L30s-40s, $100-175.

1933. Kingsbury, c. L30s-40s, $100-175.
1934. Kingsbury, c. L30s-40s, $100-175.

1935. Kingsbury, c. L30s-40s, $100-175.
1936. Kingsbury, c. L30s-40s, $100-175.

1937. Knapstein, c. 40s-E50s, $175-250.

1938. Knapstein, c. 40s-E50s, $175-250.

1939. Jacob Leinenkugels, c. L30s, $175-250.

1940. Leidiger, c. 34-40, $250+.

1941. West Bend Lithia, c. 40s, $175-250.
1942. West Bend Lithia, c. 40s, $175-250.

1943. Marathon, c. 36-39, $175-250.
1944. Marathon, c. 36-39, $100-175.

1945. Dahlke, c. 34-43, $175-250.

1946. Marshfield, c. 40s-E50s, $175-250.

1947. Electric City, c. L40s, $175-250.

1948. Electric City, c. L40s, $100-175.

1949. Miller, c. 36-40, $50-100.
1950. Miller, c. 36-40, $50-100.
1951. Miller, c. 41-L40s, $25-50.

1952. Miller, c. 40s, $50-100.

1953. Miller, c. L30s, $100-175.

1954. Mineral Spring, c. 47, $175-250.

1955. Mineral Spring, c. 40s-E50s, $100-175.
1956. Mineral Spring, c. 40s-E50s, $100-175.

1957. Mathie Ruder, c. 34-45, $175-250.

1958. Oconto, c. 48, $100-175.

1959. Cassville, c. 36-38, $100-175.

1960. Zieglers, c. 46-48, $175-250.

1961. Reedsburg, c. 41-47, $175-250.

1962. Rahr-Green Bay, c. 40s, $100-175.

1963. Rahr-Green Bay, c. 40s, $100-175.
1964. Rahr-Green Bay, c. 40s, $100-175.

1965. Rahr-Green Bay, c. 40s, $175-250.

1966. Old Port, c. 40s, $175-250.

1967. G. Heileman, c. 36-40, $100-175.

1968. G. Heileman, c. 36, $100-175.
1969. G. Heileman, c. 40s, $100-175.
1970. G. Heileman, c. 40s, $100-175.

1971. G. Heileman, c. 40s, $50-100.

1974. Denmark, c. 40, $100-175.

1979. Pabst, c. 38-46, $175-250.
1980. Pabst, c. 41, $100-175.

1972. Fischbach, c. 36, $100-175.

1975. Pabst, c. 38-46, $50-100.
1976. Pabst, c. 38-41, $25-50.
1977. Pabst, c. 41-50, $50-100.

1973. West Bend, c. 40s, $100-175.

1978. Pabst, c. 38-46, $175-250.

1981. La Crosse, c. 47-51, $100-175.
1982. La Crosse, c. 47-51, $100-175.
1983. La Crosse, c. 47-51, $100-175.

1984. La Crosse, c. 47-51, $100-175.

1985. Peoples, c. L30s-40s, $50-100.

1986. Peoples, c. 36, $50-100.
1987. Peoples, c. L30s-40s, $100-175.
1988. Peoples, c. 36, $100-175.

1989. Perplies, c. 40s, $175-250.

1990. Cream City, c. 36-39, $100-175.

1991. G. Weber, c. 51, $100-175.
1992. G. Weber, c. 51, $100-175.

1993. Platteville, c. 37-42, $250+.

1994. Plymouth, c. 36, $100-175.

1995. Stevens Point, c. L30s, $100-175.

1996. Potosi, c. 41, $100-175.
1997. Potosi, c. 40s-E50s, $100-175.

1998. Old Port, c. L30s-E40s, $175-250.

1999. Rahr-Green Bay, c. 48, $100-175.

2000. Rahr-Green Bay, c. L30s-40s, $100-175.

2001. Mathie Ruder, c. 40s, $100-175.
2002. Mathie Ruder, c. 40s, $100-175.

2003. Rhinelander, c. 48, $100-175.
2004. Rhinelander, c. 48, $100-175.
2005. Rhinelander, c. 48, $100-175.

2006. Jos. Schlitz, c. L30s, $50-100.
2007. Jos. Schlitz, c. L30s, $50-100.

2008. Wausau, c. 34-61, $100-175.
2009. Wausau, c. 34-61, $100-175.

2010. Farmers, c. 40s, $175-250.

2011. Storck, c. 35, $250+.

2012. Star, c. 36-45, $175-250.

2013. Star, c. 36-45, $175-250.

2014. Storck, c. 40s, $250+.

2015. Storck, c. 40s, $175-250.

2016. Marathon City, c. 40s-E50s, $175-250.

2017. Burlington, c. 39, $175-250.

2018. Walter, c. 40s-E50s, $100-175.

2019. Walter, c. 40s-E50s, $100-175.

2020. Walter, c. 40s-E50s, $175-250.
2021. Walter, c. 40s-E50s, $100-175.

2022. Walter, c. 40s-E50s, $100-175.

2023. Weber Waukesha, c. 40s, $100-175.

2024. Weber Waukesha, c. 42, $100-175.
2025. Weber Waukesha, c. 40s, $100-175.
2026. Weber Waukesha, c. 40s, $100-175.

2027. Two Rivers, c. 40, $175-250.
2028. Two Rivers, c. 40, $100-175.

2029. Burlington, c. 35-39, $175-250.

2030. Louis Ziegler, c. 35-39, $175-250.
2031. Louis Ziegler, c. 35-39, $175-250.

Wyoming

1935-3
1945-3
1949-2

2032. Sheridan, c. 34-38, $250+.

Foreign Breweries

2033. Amstel, Holland, c. L40s-E50s, $25-50.

2034. Atlantis, England?, c. L40s-E50s, $25-50.

2035. Beck's, Germany, c. L40s-E50s, $25-50.

2036. Black Horse, Canada, c. L30s-E50s, $25-50.

2037. Bonn, Germany, c. L40s-E50s, $25-50.

2038. Carta Blanca, Mexico, c. L40s-E50s, $25-50.

2039. Corona, Mexico, c. L40s-E50s, $25-50.

2040. DAB, Germany, c. L40s-E50s, $25-50.

2041. Deldt, Germany, c. L40s-E50s, $25-50.

2042. Dormunder, Germany, c. L40s-E50s, $25-50.

2043. Dormunder, Germany, c. L40s-E50s, $25-50.

2044. Erltes, Germany, c. L40s-E50s, $25-50.

2045. Hackerbrau, Germany, c. L40s-E50s, $25-50.

2046. Hackerbrau, Germany, c. L40s-E50s, $25-50.

2047. Heineken's, Holland, c. L40s-E50s, $25-50.

2048. Heineken's, Holland, c. L40s-E50s, $25-50.

2049. Klaver, Holland, c. L40s-E50s, $25-50.

2050. Labatt's, Canada, c. L30s-E50s, $25-50.

2051. Labatt's, Canada, c. L30s-E50s, $25-50.

2052. Lalnator, Canada, c. L30s-E50s, $25-50.

2053. Lowenbrau, Germany, c. L40s-E50s, $25-50.

2054. Munich Kindl, Germany, c. L40s-E50s, $25-50.

2055. Nuremberg, Germany, c. L40s-E50s, $25-50.

2056. O'Keefe's, Canada, c. L40s-E50s, $25-50.

2057. O'Keefe's, Canada, c. L40s-E50s, $25-50.

2058. Okocimski, Poland, c. L40s-E50s, $25-50.

2059. Paulanerbrau, Germany, c. L40s-E50s, $25-50.

2060. Pilsner Urquell, Czechoslovakia, c. L40s-E50s, $25-50.

2061. Pschorr, Germany, c. L40s-E50s, $25-50.

2062. Pschorr, Germany, c. L40s-E50s, $25-50.

2063. Sandlerbrau, Germany, c. L40s-E50s, $25-50.

2064. St. Pauli, Germany, c. L40s-E50s, $25-50.

2065. Wurzburger, Germany, c. L40s-E50s, $25-50.
2066. Wurzburger, Germany, c. L40s-E50s, $25-50.

Chapter Four

Other '30s, '40s and '50s Era Tap Markers

Other configurations than the "ball" style knobs shown in Chapter Three were used by breweries during the post-Prohibition period. Because of space limitations, the knob types discussed below were withheld from this edition. Each of the styles presented are also from the ball knob era covering the period 1933 through the mid 1950s. Many of the forms were alternatives offered by knob companies to entice breweries to use something different than ball style knobs to meet the requirement to identify the beer sold on tap.

Daka-Ware

Daka-Ware, shown in Figure 32, was a style consisting of a spherical Bakelite body to which was affixed a curved plate, made of brass or aluminum and held in place with small nails. This classic round knob with the formed metal insert was one of the earliest styles produced after Prohibition. The company usually embossed the Daka-Ware name on the side of the black Bakelite body. Green Duck later acquired this company in the 1930s and apparently ceased production of this style, continuing to make only the traditional style of ball knob. These are one of the more desirable styles of tap markers made.

Figure 32. Daka-Ware knob.

"Tin" Cans

The common nickname of "Tin Cans" certainly befits this style of knob, shown in Figure 33. Widely used by breweries, they were manufactured in large quantities by American Emblem and are characterized by a large, acetate face and hollow chrome body. The larger face was probably a desirable advertising feature at the time. The lack of durability of the acetate face made this style less sturdy over time.

Figure 33. "Tin Can" knob.

Newman Glass Faucet Knobs

Made of glass, the highly collectible and rare faucet knobs shown in Figures 34 and 35 are from the J.E. Newman Company and were produced for only one year in 1936. They were available in six (or seven) colors and enamel paint was used to imprint the brand information. Through the use of conversion kits, taverns could switch from conventional style ball knobs to the fancy glass Newman knobs. Unfortunately, this style was more expensive to manufacture than traditional knobs. In addition, they were very susceptible to breakage and the enamel lettering tended to wear off quickly, leaving a less attractive knob. This type of knob was employed primarily for Eastern brands, although some are found used with Midwest beers.

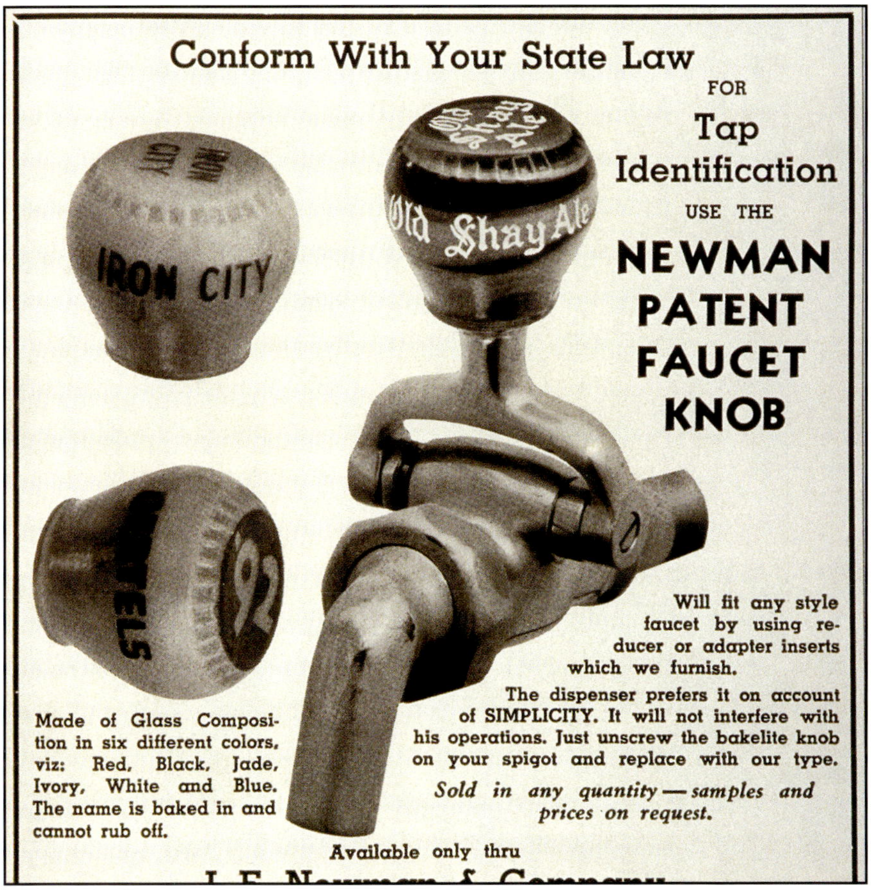

Figure 34. Newman ad, c. 1936.

Figure 35. Selection of Newman glass knobs.

Newman Aluminum

Figure 36 shows an aluminum cone-shaped knob made by Newman in the late 1930s. It likely came as a replacement for the fragile and expensive glass knobs from Newman discussed above. Like the glass knobs, these were mostly used by East Coast breweries and never did catch on as a type used on a national basis. The unusual cone shape was probably not an attractive tap marker device and offered little space for graphics. It does not appear that the Newman Company ever made a classic "ball" style knob.

Figure 36. Newman aluminum knob.

Kooler-Keg "Sidewinders"

This style of knob is unique to the Kooler-Keg system. It employed a tap marker that angled out from the keg. The chrome square rod was positioned in such a manner that the wording on the knob was parallel to the bar's surface when attached to the keg. This style has been nicknamed the "sidewinder" and an example is shown in Figure 37.

Figure 37. "Sidewinder" knob.

By June of 1939, Kooler-Keg claimed to be associated with more than two hundred leading breweries serving more than five thousand taprooms. The Kooler-Keg did not screw onto the tap handle, but rather slid onto a square shaft. As previously mentioned, the square holed Kooler-Keg knobs came in a traditional size as well as the squat version shown in Figure 38.

Figure 38. Squat version of Kooler-Keg knobs.

Other Types of Ball Knobs

Spherical Glass and Metal Balls

Glass balls employed a traditional molding process followed by an imprinting of various text with enamel paint. An example of a knob from Rooney's (owner of the Pittsburgh Steelers at the time) is shown in Figure 39.

Figure 39. Spherical glass knob.

Some manufacturers made metal ball knobs, an example of which is shown in Figure 40. Neither the glass nor the metal round knobs incorporated a stem. They never gained popularity because of cost and durability in the case of the glass knobs and ease of manufacture for the metal knobs. The opportunity for creative design in glass or metal knobs was very limited, much like with the glass and aluminum Newman knobs.

Figure 40. Spherical metal knob.

Figurals-Character Knobs

Character knobs were produced during the tap marker era. These highly collectible and fairly rare knobs are included because they provide a transition from the ball knob era. The character knob example from Old Reading Brewing, shown in Figure 41, represents the familiar figure of "Old Gus," used widely by the brewery for years.

Figure 41. Old Reading's "Gus."

Tap Marker Signs

In lieu of using ball type tap markers, the regulations permitted taverns to identify the beer being dispensed through the use of a sign, often referred to as a tap marker sign. Some of the "mystery" companies in Appendix B may have been the source for these signs. Figure 42 shows an example from Old Town Brewing. These interesting signs came in a variety of sizes and shapes and are fairly rare.

Figure 42. Tap marker sign.

The Next Era

The transition from ball knobs to the tap handles commonly used in bars today passed through a very collectible phase made up of a variety of Lucite and plastic knobs like those shown in Figure 43. It is our intent that the next effort of documenting tap markers will concentrate on this style knob, as well as fill in any gaps by including knobs of the styles shown in Figures 32 to 43. Any new finds of the traditional style ball knob will also be included. Your interest and participation is most welcome and needed.

Figure 43. The "next generation" knobs.

We will end our journey through the world of "ball" style tap markers by honoring what is purported to be the last ball knob issued. The period covered began about 1933 and ended in 1957, when the "The Real McCoy" (shown in Figure 44 and also as Knob 942) was issued. What more appropriate name than this for a beer to end the era?

Figure 44. The End of the Road.

Bibliography

Anderson, Sonja and Will. *Beers, Breweries and Breweriana*. Carmel, NY, 1969.

Anderson, Will. *The Beer Book*. Princeton, NJ: Pyne Press, 1973.

Baley, George. *Back Bar Breweriana*. Gas City, IN: L-W Book Sales, 1992 and 1994.

Baley, George. *Back Bar Beer Figurines.* Atglen, PA: Schiffer Publishing Ltd., 2002.

Beer Can Collectors of America. *United States Beer Cans*. Fenton, MO: Josten Inc., 2001.

Bull, Donald A., and John Stanley. *Just for Openers*. Atglen, PA; Schiffer Publishing Ltd., 1999.

Burden, Paul. *The Beer Tray Book*. Medfield, PA: Norfield Publishing, 1992.

Cameron, Jeffrey C. *The Class Book of U.S. Beer Cans*. Souderton, PA: Class Publishing Company, 1982.

Cornell, Martyn. *Beer Memorabilia*. Edison, NY: Chartwell Books, 2000.

Cushman, Gary, et al. *New England Breweriana*. Atglen, PA: Schiffer Publishing Ltd., 2001.

Haydock, Herb and Helen. *The World Book of Beer Memorabilia*. Paducah, KY: Turner Publishing, 1997.

Kay, Robert E. *Miniature Beer Bottles & Go-Withs*. Batavia, IL: K & K Publishers, 1980.

Martells, Jack. *The Beer Can Collector's Bible*. New York, NY: Ballantine Books, 1976.

Ojala, Reino. *20 Years of American Beers – The '30s & '40s*. Minneapolis, MN: Published by Author, Winslow Printing.

Straub, Gary. *Collectible Beer Trays*. Atglen, PA: Schiffer Publishing Ltd., 1995.

Wieren, Dale P. *American Breweries II*. West Point, PA; Eastern Coast Breweriana Association, 1995.

Vetter, John, *The New WHO's WHO In Brew*. Fairfax, VA: The Pressworks, 2000.

Appendix A

Breweriana Collector Clubs

National Association of Breweriana Advertising (NABA)
John Stanley
P.O. Box 64
Chapel Hill, NC 27514-0064

Beer Can Collectors of America (BCCA)
747 Merus Ct.
Fenton, MO 63026-2092

American Breweriana Association
P.O. Box 11157
Pueblo, CO 81001-0157

Eastern Coast Breweriana Association
John Stanley,
P.O. Box 64
Chapel Hill, NC 27514-0064

Appendix B

Ball Knob Manufacturing Companies

American Emblem Co., Utica, NY
American Tap Bush Co., Detroit, MI
Bastian Bros., Rochester, NY
Bay State Moulding, Boston, MA
Central Brass Mfg. Co., Cleveland, OH
Crown Equipment Co., Newark, NJ
Daka-Ware, Chicago, IL
Eick, Otto, Inc., St. Louis, MO
Fisher Products, Inc., Syracuse, NY
Fox, Cincinnati, OH
General Products Co., Providence, RI
Green Duck Co., Chicago, IL
Hanson, C., Chicago, IL
Kooler-Keg, Belleville, NJ
Krest Mfg. Co. Inc., New York, NY
Merritt, Clark C. Co. Inc., Long Branch, NJ
New Art Specialties, Chicago, IL
Newman, J.E. & Co., Pittsburgh, PA
O'Hara Waltham Mfg., Waltham, MA
Price Bros., Chicago, IL
Robbins Co., Attleboro, MA
Selimore, city/state unknown

Index of Breweries

Brewery	City	State	Reference Numbers	In Business
Acme Brewing Co.	San Francisco	CA	8-12	1934-54
Adam Scheidt Brewing Co.	Norristown	PA	1629-1635, 1723-1729, 1750	1933-60
Adolph Coors Co.	Golden	CO	41-43	1933-49
Ajax Brewing Co.	Indianapolis	IN	330	1939-41
Akron Brewing Co.	Akron	OH	1292	1933-39
Altoona Brewing Co.	Altoona	PA	1307, 1621, 1625	1936-74
Ambrosia Brewing Co.	Chicago	IL	88-89, 217-219	1939-54
American Brewery	Baltimore	MD	366-368	1933-72
American Brewing Co.	Granite City	IL	252	1938-40
American Brewing Co.	Rochester	NY	741, 1097-1105	1933-50
American Brewing Co.	Miami	FL	76-77	1940-57
Amsterdam Brewing Co.	Amsterdam	NY	740-739, 1056	1934-39
Anheuser-Busch, Inc.	St. Louis	MO	564-570, 591-596, 600	1933-
Ann Arbor Brewing Co.	Ann Arbor	MI	483	1933-37
Arcadia Brewing Co.	Arcadia	WI	1838	1934-40
Arizona Brewing Co.	Phoenix	AZ	1-6	1933-64
Ashland Brewing Co.	Ashland	PA	1580, 1645	1935-38
Atlantic Brewing Co.	Chicago	IL	94, 118, 292-294, 1141-1142	1933-66
Atlas Brewing Co.	Chicago	IL	81-84, 95-101	1937-63
August Wagner Breweries	Columbus	OH	1146, 1196-1197	1933-74
Aurora Brewing Co.	Aurora	IL	103	1933-39
Auto City Brewing Co.	Hamtramck	MI	478	1935-43
Aztec Brewing Co.	San Diego	CA	7	1933-37
Ballantine, P. & Sons Brewing Co.	Newark	NJ	626-637	1933-71
Barbey's Inc.	Reading	PA	1688-1695	1933-70
Bartels Brewing Co.	Syracuse	NY	747-748	1933-37
Bartels Brewing Co.	Edwardsville	PA	1311-1313	1946-50
Bavarian Brewing Co.	Covington	KY	352-357, 362	1938-52
Bay City Brewing Co.	Bay City	MI	492	1934-43
Bechauds Inc.	Fon Du Lac	WI	1885	1933-41
Beck, Magnus Brewing Co.	Buffalo	NY	749-751	1936-54
Becker Products Co.	Ogden	UT	1790	1934-48
Berghoff Brewing Co.	Fort Wayne	IN	318-320	1936-54
Berlin Brewing Co.	Berlin	WI	1842-1845	1936-48
Best Brewing Co.	Chicago	IL	107-108, 147-148, 179-180	1933-50
Beth Uhl Brewing Co.	Bethlehem	PA	1359, 1699-1702, 1719	1933-41
Betz, John F. & Son	Philadelphia	PA	1320	1933-39
Beverwyck Brewery Co.	Albany	NY	752-756, 1138	1933-50
Binzel Brewing Co.	Oconomowoc	WI	1846	1936-42
Birk Brothers Brewing Co.	Chicago	IL	134, 288, 290-291, 299-301	1933-50
Birk's Brewing Co.	Chicago	IL	109	1933-35
Bismark Brewing Co.	Chicago	IL	110-111, 194-196, 221	1933-41
Blackhawk Brewing Co.	Davenport	IA	347	1944-52
Blatz Brewing Co.	Milwaukee	WI	1847-1859	1933-57
Bleser Brewing Co.	Manitowoc	WI	1860, 1881, 1906	1933-42
Blitz Weinhard Co.	Portland	OR	1297-1300	1933-59
Bloomer Brewery Inc.	Bloomer	WI	1836	1933-47
Bluff City Brewing Co.	Alton	IL	112	1933-35
Blumer Brewing Corp.	Monroe	WI	1912-1916	1933-47
Bohemian Breweries	Spokane	WA	1796	1934-59
Bohemian Brewing Co.	Joliet	IL	115-117	1950-58
Bosch Brewing Co.	Houghton	MI	479-480	1933-74
Boston Beer Co.	Boston	MA	388, 391-393	1933-57
Boyertown Brewing Co.	Boyertown	PA	1327	1933-51
Brackenridge Brewing Co.	Brackenridge	PA	1557-1558	1933-45
Breidt, Peter Brewing Co.	Elizabeth	NJ	638-643	1935-51
Brewing Company of America	Cleveland	OH	1173-1176	1934-45
Bridgeport Brewing Co.	Bridgeport	CT	60, 64-65	1933-41
Brockert Brewing Co.	Worcester	MA	398-399	1936-39
Bruckmann Co.	Cincinnati	OH	1153-1156	1933-49
Buckeye Brewing Co.	Toledo	OH	1157-1159	1933-68
Buffalo Brewing Co.	Sacramento	CA	13-15	1933-42
Burger Brewing Co.	Cincinnati	OH	1161-1166, 1262	1934-51
Burke Brewery Co.	Long Island	NY	762-767	1934-48
Burkhardt Brewing Co.	Akron	OH	1167-1169, 1223-1224	1933-57
Burlington Brewing Co.	Burlington	WI	1870-1871, 2017, 2029	1934-53
Burton Brewing Co.	Paterson	NJ	644-645, 655-658, 700-702, 734-737	1933-49
Burton Products Inc.	Union City	NJ	728-729	1935-45
Bushkill Products Co.	Easton	PA	1328-1330	1933-41

Brewery	City	State	Reference Numbers	In Business
Butte Brewing Co.	Butte	MT	602	1933-63
Calumet Brewing Co.	Chilton	WI	1872	1934-37
Cambria Brewing Co.	Johnstown	PA	1332	1934-37
Camden County Beverage Co.	Camden	NJ	646-648, 699	1934-64
Canadian Ace Brewing Co.	Chicago	IL	127-130	1947-68
Canton Brewing Co.	Canton	OH	1172	1933-37
Capitol Brewing Co.	Milwaukee	WI	1873, 1878	1934-48
Carling Brewing Co.	Belleville	IL	281	1954-75
Cassville Brewing Co.	Cassville	WI	1959	1933-38
Cataract Brewing Co.	Rochester	NY	773-774, 781, 953	1933-40
Centlivre Brewing Co.	Fort Wayne	IN	336-338	1946-60
Champ Brewing Co.	Pittston	PA	1751-1753	1946-48
Chartiers Valley Brewing Co.	Carnegie	PA	1308-1309, 1333-1335, 1417	1936-41
Chautauqua Brewing Co.	Jamestown	NY	778	1939-41
Chester Brewery Co.	Chester	PA	1337-40, 1647-1648, 1730	1934-53
City Brewing Corp.	Ridgewood	NY	912, 1093-1096	1933-50
Class & Nachod Brewing Co.	Philadelphia	PA	1449	1933-36
Cleveland Home Brewing Co.	Cleveland	OH	1151, 1186	1936-52
Cleveland-Sandusky Brewing Co.	Cleveland	OH	1182-1185, 1198-1199, 1244-1245	1933-62
Clyffside Brewing Co.	Cincinnati	OH	1193-1194	1933-45
Cold Spring Brewing Co.	Lawrence	MA	424-431, 539	1933-51
Columbia Brewing Co.	St. Louis	MO	563, 1343-1345, 1794-1795, 1797	1933-48
Columbus Brewing Co.	Columbus	NE	615	1950-63
Consumer's Brewing Co.	Newark	OH	1180, 1240, 1246-1248	1942-53
Cook, F.W. Co.	Evansville	IN	324	1933-55
Cooper Brewing Co.	York	PA	1350-1351, 1353, 1539-1540	1936-46
Cream City Brewing Co.	Milwaukee	WI	1990	1933-39
Cremo Brewing Co.	New Britain	CT	52-55, 68-69	1933-55
Crete Brewing Co.	Crete	NE	610	1936-41
Crockery City Ice & Products Co.	East Liverpool	OH	1181, 1287, 1289	1933-43
Croft Brewing Co.	Boston	MA	401-410, 423, 467-468	1934-52
Cumberland Brewing Co.	Cumberland	MD	383-384	1933-70
Daeufer-Lieberman Brewing Co.	Allentown	PA	1355-1356	1933-40
Dahlke Brewing Co.	Westfield	WI	1945	1934-43
Dawsons Brewery Co.	New Bedford	MA	411-418	1933-68
Deerpark Beverage, Inc.	Port Jervis	NY	783, 807, 1067	1934-41
Del Mar Va Brewing Co.	Wilmington	DE	73	1937-45
Delatron Brewing Co.	Reading	OH	1187	1933-46
Denmark Brewing Co.	Denmark	WI	1830, 1974	1933-47
Deppen Mfg. Co.	Reading	PA	1357-1358, 1378	1933-37
Detroit Brewing Co.	Detroit	MI	485, 515, 520-521, 531	1933-48
Diamond Spring Brewery Co.	Lawrence	MA	446-452	1934-72
Diamond State Brewing Co.	Wilmington	DE	74-75	1935-56
Dick Brothers Brewing Co.	Quincy	IL	143	1937-51
Diehl, Christ Brewing Co.	Defiance	OH	1188-1190	1933-53
Dobler Brewing Co.	Albany	NY	786-791	1933-58
Doelger, Peter Brewing Co.	Harrison	NJ	698, 715-722	1935-48
Drewerys LTD USA	South Bend	IN	325-329	1937-72
Du Bois Brewing Co.	DuBois	PA	1361-1363, 1624	1933-73
Duluth Brewing & Malting Co.	Duluth	MN	538, 553	1934-66
Duquesne Brewing Co.	Pittsburgh	PA	1364-1371, 1650-1651	1933-72
E & B Brewing Co.	Detroit	MI	486-491	1933-62
Eagle Brewing Co.	Utica	NY	808, 1336, 1562-1565	1933-64
Eastern Brewing Co.	Hammonton	NJ	669-671, 675, 703	1939-72
Eastside Brewing Co.	Los Angeles	CA	18	1934-54
Eberhardt & Ober Brewery Co.	Pittsburgh	PA	1372-1376, 1379-1380	1935-52
Eberle Brewing Co., Inc.	Jackson	MI	508	1933-41
Ebling Brewing Co.	New York	NY	809-815, 884, 1086, 1135-1136	1933-51
Ebner, Carl Brewing Co.	Fort Atkinson	WI	1882	1933-46
Edelbrau Brewery Co.	Brooklyn	NY	816-823, 869-873, 1036-1037	1940-51
Edelbrew Brewing Co.	Brooklyn	NY	825-828, 903	1946-57
Effinger Co.	Baraboo	WI	1883-1884	1934-37
Ehret, Geo. Brewery Co.	Brooklyn	NY	829-836	1933-48
Eichler, John Brewing Co.	New York	NY	837	1933-47
Eilert Brewing Co.	Cleveland	OH	1191	1934-39
Eldredge Brewing Co.	Portsmouth	NH	621	1933-40
Electric City Brewing Co.	Kaukauna	WI	1947-1948	1933-48
Empire State Brewery	Olean	NY	801-803, 840, 956, 965	1934-40
Enterprise Brewing Co.	Fall River	MA	390, 457-458, 460	1940-50
Erie Brewing Co.	Erie	PA	1497, 1561	1933-64
Erlanger, Otto Brewing Co.	Philadelphia	PA	1381-1384, 1619	1936-53
Essex Brewing Co.	Haverhill	MA	422	1935-38
Esslingers, Inc.	Philadelphia	PA	1385-1392	1934-77
Eulberg Brewing Co.	Portage	WI	1886	1938-57
Falls City Brewing Co.	Louisville	KY	358	1933-47
Falstaff Brewing Co.	St. Louis	MO	577-579	1933-58

Brewery	City	State	Reference Numbers	In Business
Farmers Brewing Co.	Shawano	WI	2010	1935-48
Fauerbach Brewing Co.	Madison	WI	1887-1889	1933-66
Fecker Brewing Co.	Danville	IL	158	1933-39
Feigenspan, Christian Brewing Co.	Newark	NJ	650-654	1933-56
Fell Brewing Co.	Carbondale	PA	1397-1398	1933-51
Ferwood Brewing Co.	Lansdowne	PA	1432-1433	1933-41
Fesenmeier Brewing Co.	Huntington	WV	1829	1936-49
Fidelio Brewing Co.	New York	NY	842, 943-946	1935-48
Fischbach Brewing Co.	Milwaukee	WI	1972	1933-36
Fisher Brewing Co.	Salt Lake City	UT	1791	1933-60
Fitger Brewing Co.	Duluth	MN	540-542	1933-72
Fitzgerald Brothers Brewing Co.	Troy	NY	843-851	1933-56
Flock Brewing Co.	Williamsport	PA	1399-1403, 1620	1933-50
Fontenelle Brewing Co.	Omaha	NE	612, 614	1933-38
Food City Brewing Co.	Battle Creek	MI	482	1933-40
Forest City Brewery	Cleveland	OH	1282-1284	1933-45
Fort Pitt Brewing Co.	Jeannette	PA	1405-1408, 1595-1597	1936-54
Fort Stanwix Brewing Co.	Rome	NY	856	1935-37
Fortune Bros. Brewing Co.	Chicago	IL	159-161, 268	1933-49
Fountain Brewing Co.	Fountain City	WI	1891	1933-66
Fox Deluxe Brewing Co.	Grand Rapids	MI	493	1950-53
Fox Head Waukesha Corp.	Waukesha	WI	1892-1894	1935-47
Fox Lake Brewing Co.	Fox Lake	WI	1895	1934-37
Fox Valley Brewing Co.	Menasha	WI	1890, 1896	1934-41
Fox, Peter Brewing Co.	Chicago	IL	162-164, 227, 277	1933-55
Frankenmuth Brewing Co.	Frankenmuth	MI	494-499	1936-54
Franklin Brewing Co.	Columbus	OH	1148-1150	1934-56
Franklin Brewing Co.	Hanover	PA	1409-1411	1934-56
Fredericks Brewing Co.	Thornton	IL	226	1935-41
Free State Brewing Co.	Baltimore	MD	371, 387	1933-50
Freeland Brewing Co.	Freeland	PA	1412-1413	1933-40
Freimanns Beverage & Ice Co.	Upper Sandusky	OH	1238	1934-46
Fresno Brewing Co.	Fresno	CA	30	1933-40
Fritz Brewing Co.	Freeport	IL	165	1933-37
Frontier Brewery Co.	Tonawanda	NY	779-780, 934-936	1935-48
Fuhrmann & Schmidt Brewing Co.	Shamokin	PA	1393-1396	1934-75
Galena Brewing Co.	Galena	IL	251	1933-35
Galveston-Houston Brewing Co.	Galveston	TX	1789	1933-55
Gambrinus Brewing Co.	Chicago	IL	166	1933-35
Garden City Brewing Co.	Chicago	IL	154-155, 167-168, 222-224, 235, 246-247	1933-51
Gast Brewery Inc.	St. Louis	MO	580	1934-46
Gast Brewing Co.	Highland	IL	169	1947-49
Gateway Brewing Co.	Clinton	IA	348-349	1940-41
General Braddock Brewing Co.	Braddock	PA	1639	1933-37
General Brewing Co.	San Francisco	CA	28	1933-48
Genesee Brewing Co.	Rochester	NY	785, 857-867, 971	1933-64
Gerhard Lang Brewery Co.	Buffalo	NY	886-889, 913-916, 955	1933-49
German Brewing Co.	Cumberland	MD	385-386	1933-41
Gerst, Wm. Brewing Co.	Nashville	TN	1784	1936-53
Gettelmann, A. Brewing Co.	Milwaukee	WI	1900-1905	1933-62
Geyer Brothers Brewery	Frankenmuth	MI	502	1933-90
Gipps Brewing Co.	Peoria	IL	170-172	1933-54
Globe Brewing Co.	Baltimore	MD	369-370	1933-63
Gluek Brewing Co.	Minneapolis	MN	543-544	1933-65
Goebel Brewing Co.	Detroit	MI	503-507	1933-63
Goenner & Co.	Johnstown	PA	1416, 1428-1431, 1554-1555	1936-53
Goetz, M.K. Brewing Co.	St. Joseph	MO	572-576	1933-60
Golden Age Brewery Co.	Spokane	WA	1804-1805	1934-48
Golden West Brewing Co.	Oakland	CA	22-23	1933-38
Goldenrod Brewing Co.	Brooklyn	NY	824, 1035	1942-44
Grace Bros. Brewing Co.	Santa Rosa	CA	25-27	1933-51
Grand Valley Brewing Co.	Ionia	MI	500-501	1933-37
Graupner, Robt. Inc.	Harrisburg	PA	1434-1442, 1483-1484, 1649,1718	1933-51
Greater New York Brewery Co.	Ridgewood	NY	745-746, 874, 1074, 1131	1946-50
Green Bay Brewing Co.	Green Bay	WI	1835	1934-36
Greenway Brewery Co.	Syracuse	NY	875-879	1936-52
Gretz, Wm. Brewing Co.	Philadelphia	PA	1443-1448	1933-61
Griesedieck Bros. Brewing Co.	St. Louis	MO	581-584	1933-59
Gunthers Brewing Co.	Baltimore	MD	372	1938-60
Haas, A. A. Brewing Co.	Houghton	MI	509	1933-42
Haberle Congress Brewing Co.	Syracuse	NY	757-758, 782, 784, 880	1933-62
Haefner Brewing Co.	Lancaster	PA	1450, 1574, 1581, 1642	1934-40
Haffenreffer & Co.	Boston	MA	394-397, 461-466	1933-54
Hamm, Theo. Brewing Co.	St. Paul	MN	548-552	1933-75
Hampden Brewing Co.	Willimansett	MA	432-438	1933-57
Hanley, James Inc.	Providence	RI	1763-1768, 1782	1934-57

Brewery	City	State	Reference Numbers	In Business
Harvard Brewing Co.	Lowell	MA	400, 439-445	1933-57
Hawaii Brewing Co.	Honolulu	HI	78	1933-44
Heidelberg Brewing Co.	Covington	KY	351, 363	1934-49
Heileman, G. Brewing Co.	La Crosse	WI	1967-1971	1933-97
Helbs Keystone Brewery	York	PA	1342, 1454	1934-36
Hemrich Brewing Co.	Seattle	WA	1806	1934-39
Hendrick Brewing Co.	Albany	NY	797, 881-883	1934-56
Hennrich Brewing Co.	Seattle	WA	1807	1934-39
Hensler, Jos. Brewing Co.	Newark	NJ	659-665	1933-37
Heurich, Chr. Brewing Co.	Washington	DC	72	1940-48
Highland Spring Brewing Co.	Highland Spring	MA	473	1933-33
Hillsboro Brewing Co.	Hillsboro	WI	1918	1937-43
Hochgreve Brewing Co.	Green Bay	WI	1920-1921	1933-49
Hocking Valley Brewing Co.	Nelsonville	OH	1201	1936-47
Hoerber Brewing Co.	Chicago	IL	140-141, 182, 243, 311	1933-41
Hofbrau Brewing Co.	Allentown	PA	1456	1933-73
Hoffman Beverage Co.	Newark	NJ	666-668	1934-46
Hohenadel, John Brewery Inc.	Philadelphia	PA	1457-1460, 1477	1936-52
Holihan Bros. Brewing Co.	Lawrence	MA	419-421	1934-72
Hollen Brewing Co.	Hillsgrove	RI	1769	1936-38
Home Brewing Co.	Richmond	VA	1793	1934-69
Homestead Ice Co.	West Homestead	PA	1455, 1461-1463, 1531	1934-53
Horlacher Brewing Co.	Allentown	PA	1464-1468	1933-51
Horluck Brewing Co.	Seattle	WA	1828	1936-39
Hornell Brewing Co.	Hornell	NY	885, 904, 968-969, 1062-1063	1933-64
Hornung, Jacob Brewing Co.	Philadelphia	PA	1469-1476, 1522	1934-53
Horton Pilsener Brewing Co.	New York	NY	890-893, 966, 970	1933 40
Howell & King Co.	Pittston	PA	1618	1934-39
Huber, Jos. Brewing Co.	Monroe	WI	1922	1947-
Hudepohl Brewing Co.	Cincinnati	OH	1202-1211	1933-77
Hull Brewing Co.	New Haven	CT	56-59	1933-77
Huntley Brewing Co.	Huntley	IL	104	1934-38
Hupfel, J Chr G. Brewing Co.	New York	NY	894	1933-38
Hyde Park Brewing Assn.	St. Louis	MO	585-590	1936-54
Illinois Brewing Co.	Thornton	IL	157, 183, 236, 241, 249	1935-41
Independent Milwaukee Brewery Co.	Milwaukee	WI	1863-1867, 1923	1933-64
Iroquois Beverage Co.	Buffalo	NY	900-901	1933-55
Jackson Brewing Co.	New Orleans	LA	365, 1263	1938-66
Jacob Ruppert	New York	NY	962-964, 1038-1055	1933-66
Jenner Springs Brewing Co.	Boswell	PA	1323	1933-38
Johnson, Harold C. Brewing Co.	Lomira	WI	1874	1949-53
Joliet Citizens Brewing Co.	Joliet	IL	114, 136-138, 231	1933-48
Jones Brewing Co.	Smithton	PA	1677-1682	1933-
Jones, Frank Brewing Co.	Portsmouth	NH	619-620	1933-50
Jung, Wm. G. Brewing Co.	Randon Lake	WI	1925-1929	1936-54
Kaier, Chas. D. Co.	Mahanoy City	PA	1485-1494	1933-68
Kamm & Schellinger Co.	Mishawaka	IN	332-335	1936-52
Keeley Brewing Co.	Chicago	IL	186-192	1933-46
Kern Brewing Co.	Bakersfield	CA	31	1934-40
Kewaunee Brewing Co.	Kewaunee	WI	1841	1933-42
Keystone Brewing Co.	Scranton	PA	1495-1496	1935-36
Kiewel Brewing Co.	Little Falls	MN	554	1933-60
Kiley Brewing Co.	Marion	IN	339-341	1933-41
Kings Brewery	Brooklyn	NY	760-761, 1171, 1212	1939-41
Kings Tavern Brewing Co.	Flint	MI	510	1938-39
Kingsbury Brewery Co.	Manitowoc	WI	1930-1936	1934-49
Kips Bay Brewing Co.	New York	NY	905-909, 1073, 1075	1933-48
Kling, PH Brewing Co.	Flint	MI	511	1934-48
Knapstein Brewing Co.	New London	WI	1937-1938	1933-50
Koch, Fred Brewery Co.	Dunkirk	NY	910-911	1933-89
Koerber Brewing Co.	Toledo	OH	1213-1214, 1243, 1280	1933-48
Kolb Brewing Co.	Bay City	MI	512	1933-43
Koller Brewing Co.	Chicago	IL	197, 298	1936-52
Koppitz-Melchers	Detroit	MI	513-514	1933-47
Krantz Brewing Co.	Findlay	OH	1231-1233	1944-56
Krueger, G. Brewing Co.	Newark	NJ	677-697	1939-60
Kuebler Brewing Co.	Easton	PA	1498-1506	1936-53
La Crosse Brewery Co.	La Crosse	WI	1981-1984	1947-51
Lackawanna Beer and Ale Corp.	Scranton	PA	1507	1933-43
Lafayette Brewing Co.	Lafayette	IN	346	1936-53
Lancaster Breweries Inc.	Lancaster	OH	1170, 1195, 1268	1934-42
Largay Brewing Co.	Waterbury	CT	61, 66-67	1933-44
Latrobe Brewing Co.	Latrobe	PA	1310, 1508-1511, 1638	1934-40
Lebanon Brewing Co.	Lebanon	PA	1512-1517	1936-52
Lebanon Valley Brewing Co.	Lebanon	PA	1304, 1573	1933-52
Leidiger Brewing Co.	Merrill	WI	1940	1934-40

Brewery	City	State	Reference Numbers	In Business
Leinenkugels, Jacob Brewing Co.	Chippewa Falls	WI	1939	1933-87
Leisy Brewing Co.	Cleveland	OH	1215-1217	1933-61
Lemp, Wm. J. Brewing Co.	East St. Louis	IL	198-199	1939-42
Liebert & Obert Brewing Co.	Manayunk	PA	1346-1349, 1352, 1518-1519, 1526	1936-46
Liebmann Brewery Co.	Brooklyn	NY	917-918, 959-961, 1023-1034, 1064-1065	1933-64
Linden Brewery Co.	Linderhurst	NY	919-923	1938-47
Lion Brewery Co.	New York	NY	868, 924-929, 1130, 1132	1933-41
Lion, The Inc.	Wilkes-Barre	PA	1420-1425, 1578-1579	1934-72
Lockport Brewing Co.	Lock Haven	PA	1341, 1418-1419, 1521, 1566	1933-44
Loewers Brewing Co.	New York	NY	930-933	1933-47
Lone Star Brewing Co.	San Antonio	TX	1786	1941-70
Los Angeles Brewing Co.	Los Angeles	CA	17	1933-37
Louis Eckert Brewing Co.	Los Angeles	CA	19	1933-43
Lubeck Brewing Co.	Toledo	OH	1219	1933-39
Maier Brewing Co.	Los Angeles	CA	29	1935-71
Malt Marrow Brewing Co.	Chicago	IL	202	1935-38
Manhattan Brewing Co.	Chicago	IL	85, 124-126, 203-204, 230	1933-68
Marathon Brewing Co.	Marathon	WI	1943-1944	1933-39
Marathon City Brewing Co.	Marathon	WI	2016	1933-68
Marshfield Brewing Co.	Marshfield	WI	1946	1933-66
Mathie Ruder Brewing Co.	Wausau	WI	1910, 1957, 2001-2002	1934-54
Matz Brewing Co.	Bellaire	OH	1143-1144	1935-54
Mauch Chunk Brewing Co.	East Mauch Chunk	PA	1414-1415	1933-41
McAvoy Brewing Co.	Thornton	IL	206	1948-49
McCoy Corp.	Buffalo	NY	942	1954-57
McDermott Brewing Co.	Chicago	IL	123	1933-37
McHenry Brewing Co.	McHenry	IL	207	1934-43
Menominee-Marinette Brewing Co.	Menominee	MI	516	1936-54
Metz Brewing Co.	Omaha	NE	611, 613	1939-63
Miami Valley Brewing Co.	Dayton	OH	1218	1933-50
Michigan Brewing Co.	Grand Rapids	MI	481	1936-39
Milan Brewing Co.	Milan	OH	1220, 1266	1933-50
Miller Brewing Co.	Milwaukee	WI	1949-1953	1933-
Milwaukee Brewery of San Francisco	San Francisco	CA	24	1935-50
Mineral Spring Brewing Co.	Mineral Point	WI	1954-1956	1933-60
Minneapolis Brewing Co.	Minneapolis	MN	545-547	1946-56
Mission Brewing Co.	Los Angeles	CA	32-33	1934-54
Missoula Brewing Co.	Missoula	MT	605-609	1933-65
Mitchell, Harry Brewing Co.	El Paso	TX	1785	1933-42
Monarch Brewing Co.	Chicago	IL	102, 119, 149-152, 212-216	1933-58
Moore & Quinn	Syracuse	NY	899, 949, 1010	1937-50
Moose Brewing Co.	Roscoe	PA	1324-1326, 1529-1530, 1616-1617	1933-49
Mound City Brewing Co.	Mound City	IL	205, 248	1933-50
Mount Carmel Brewery Co.	Mount Carmel	PA	1305, 1321, 1528, 1537	1939-51
Mt. Carbon Brewery Co.	Pottsville	PA	1306, 1314-1318, 1360, 1532-1536, 1560, 1567-1569, 1575-1577	1933-77
Muehlebach, George Brewing Co.	Kansas City	MO	597-599	1934-56
Mutual Brewing Co.	Ellensburg	WA	1803, 1811	1934-43
Narragansett Brewing Co.	Cranston	RI	1762, 1770-1781	1933-66
National Brewing Co.	Baltimore	MD	373-382, 1585	1933-39
Nectar Brewing Co.	Elmira	NY	838-839, 1066	1933-38
Neuweiler, Louis F. & Sons	Allentown	PA	1541-1553, 1556	1933-62
New Brunswick Brewing Co.	New Brunswick	NJ	649, 672-674	1935-38
New England Brewing Co.	Hartford	CT	63	1933-48
New Philadelphia Brewery Co.	New Philadelphia	OH	1226, 1239, 1242, 1559	1936-49
North American Brewing Co.	Brooklyn	NY	792-793, 796, 895-896, 898, 981	1933-46
Northampton Brewery Co.	Northampton	PA	1570-1571, 1710-1715, 1740-1746	1933-50
Northern Brewing Co.	Watertown	NY	902, 1133-1134	1933-48
Oconto Brewing Co.	Oconto	WI	1958	1938-65
Oertel Brewing Co.	Louisville	KY	359-360	1935-64
Ohio Brewery	Columbus	OH	1152, 1296	1933-48
Old Abbey Brewing Co.	Chicago	IL	220	1935-41
Old Capitol Brewing Co.	Chillicothe	OH	1227-1228	1934-47
Old Dutch Breweries Inc	Brooklyn	NY	759, 950-952, 1119	1934-48
Old Indian Brewing Co.	Indian	PA	1582	1936-38
Old Lancaster Brewing Co.	Lancaster	PA	1610	1933-38
Old Port Brewing Co.	Port Washington	WI	1966, 1998	1933-48
Old Reading Brewery Co.	Reading	PA	1319, 1586-1593	1933-69
Old Reliable Brewing Co.	Greensburg	PA	1594	1938-41
Olt Bros. Brewing Co.	Dayton	OH	1249	1933-41
Olympia Brewing Co.	Olympia	WA	1812-1813	1933-
Oneida Brewing Co.	Utica	NY	979	1933-42
Ortlieb, Henry F. Brewing Co.	Philadelphia	PA	1611-1614	1933-89
Oshkosh Brewing Co.	Oshkosh	WI	1875-1877	1936-71
Overland Beverage Co.	Nampa	ID	80	1934-50
Pabst Brewing Co.	Milwaukee	WI	1837, 1975-1980	1939-83

Brewery	City	State	Reference Numbers	In Business
Pacific Malting & Brewing Co.	San Jose	CA	20, 39	1936-52
Patrick Henry Brewing Co.	Chicago	IL	184	1936-39
Peerless Brewing Co.	Washington	MO	571	1934-40
Penn Star Brewing Co.	Lancaster	PA	1615, 1636-1637	1933-59
Peoples Brewing Co.	Oshkosh	WI	1985-1988	1935-74
Peoples Brewing Co.	Duluth	MN	555, 676, 704-705, 731-732	1933-52
Peoria Brewing Co.	Peoria	IL	135, 305	1933-47
Perplies Brewing Co.	Jefferson	WI	1924, 1989	1934-52
Peter Barmann Brewery	Kingston	NY	742-744, 841	1933-41
Peter Hand Brewery	Chicago	IL	208-211, 238-240	1933-68
Peter, Wm. Brewing Co.	Union City	NJ	622-625, 706-714	1933-48
Pfeiffer Brewing Co.	Detroit	MI	522-525	1933-58
Philadelphia Brewing Co.	Philadelphia	PA	1524-1527, 1598-1609	1933-49
Phoenix Brewery Co.	Bay City	MI	526	1935-39
Phoenix Brewery Corp.	Buffalo	NY	947-948, 957-958, 982-985	1933-59
Piel Brothers Brewing Co.	Brooklyn	NY	986-1001	1933-73
Pilsen Brewing Co.	Chicago	IL	234, 304, 312-314	1933-61
Pilsener Brewing Co.	Cleveland	OH	1250-1255, 1278	1933-63
Pilsener Brewing Co.	Hazelton	PA	1451-1453	1933-50
Pilser Brewing Co.	New York	NY	1002-1006	1934-48
Pioneer Brewing Co.	Joliet	IL	242	1934-48
Pioneer Brewing Co.	Walla Walla	WA	1816	1944-48
Pioneer Brewing Co.	Aberdeen	WA	1814-1815	1933-44
Pittsburgh Brewing Co.	Pittsburgh	PA	1322, 1478-1482, 1583, 1654, 1703-1707	1933-46
Pittston Brewing Co.	Pittston	PA	1377, 1426-1427, 1584	1934-42
Platteville Brewing Co.	Platteville	WI	1993	1937-42
Plymouth Brewing Co.	Plymouth	WI	1994	1933-38
Poth Brewery Co.	Philadelphia	PA	1626-1628	1937-41
Potosi Brewing Co.	Potosi	WI	1996-1997	1933-72
Power City Brewing Co.	Niagara Falls	NY	1007	1937-40
Premier Brewing Co.	Fergus Falls	MN	556	1933-36
Prima Brewing Co.	Chicago	IL	105-106, 175-176, 259, 295-297, 307	1935-41
Prima-Bismark Brewing Co.	Chicago	IL	185, 193, 244-245	1933-41
Quandt Brewing Co.	Troy	NY	1008-1009, 1137	1933-41
Rahr-Green Bay Brewing Corp.	Green Bay	WI	1962-1965, 1999-2000	1934-66
Rainier Brewing Co.	San Francisco	CA	34-35, 38	1934-53
Red Top Brewing Co.	Cincinnati	OH	1145, 1147, 1256-1258	1933-56
Reedsburg Brewery	Reedsburg	WI	1961	1941-47
Regal Amber Brewing Co.	San Francisco	CA	36-37	1934-53
Reisch Brewing Co.	Springfield	IL	253-254	1933-67
Renner & Weber Brewing Co.	Mansfield	OH	1291	1933-51
Renner Co.	Youngstown	OH	1177-1179, 1241, 1259-1261	1933-62
Renner, Geo. J. Brewing Co.	Akron	OH	1200, 1229-1230, 1235-1236, 1269-1270	1935-53
Reno Brewing Co.	Reno	NV	617-618	1933-58
Rhinelander Brewery Co.	Rhinelander	WI	2003-2005	1934-68
Rheinlander Brewery Inc.	Seattle	WA	1819	1933-44
Rice Lake Brewing Co.	Rice Lake	WI	1868-1869	1933-71
Rio Grande Brewing Corp.	Albuquerque	NM	738	1937-39
Rochester Brewing Co.	Rochester	NY	972-977, 980, 1106-1107	1933-56
Rock Island Brewing Co.	Rock Island	IL	142, 229, 265	1933-39
Roosevelt Brewing Co.	Chicago	IL	113, 131, 264	1933-38
Rubsam & Horrmann Brewing Co.	Staten Island	NY	1011-1022	1936-53
Ruff-Reidel Brewing Co.	Quincy	IL	139, 269	1933-48
Salem Brewing Assn.	Salem	OR	1303	1934-44
San Antonio Brewing Assn.	San Antonio	TX	1787	1936-52
San Francisco Brewing Co.	San Francisco	CA	16	1935-57
Schaefer, Chas. Corp.	Brooklyn	NY	794-795, 897	1946-48
Schaefer, F & M Brewing Co.	Brooklyn	NY	1057-1059	1933-76
Schiller Brewing Co.	Philadelphia	PA	1643	1940-41
Schlitz, Jos. Brewing Co.	Milwaukee	WI	2006-2007	1933-98
Schmidt Jacob Brewing Co.	St. Paul	MN	557-562	1933-62
Schmidt, C. & Sons, Inc.	Philadelphia	PA	1644	1933-88
Schmidt, K.G. Brewing Co.	Logansport	IN	342	1936-53
Schmidt's Brewing Co.	Detroit	MI	527-529	1936-53
Schneider, Ph. Brewing Co.	Trinadad	CO	40, 44	1933-55
Schoenhofen Edelweiss Co.	Chicago	IL	144-146, 261-263	1934-71
Schoenling Brewing Co.	Cincinnati	OH	1265, 1279	1934-74
Schott Brewing Co.	Highland	IL	181, 271	1933-47
Schreiber Brewing Co.	Buffalo	NY	937-940, 1060-1061	1933-50
Schultz Brewing Co.	Union City	NJ	724-727	1935-45
Seattle Brewing & Malting Co.	Seattle	WA	1820, 1822-1824	1935-56
Sebewaing Brewing Co.	Sebewaing	MI	517-519	1938-45
Seeber Brewing Co.	Elizabeth	NJ	730	1934-38
Seitz Brewing Co.	Easton	PA	1646	1933-39
Semrad-Pusch	Highland	WI	1917	1933-42
Sheridan Brewing Co.	Sheridan	WY	2032	1934-38

Brewery	City	State	Reference Numbers	In Business
Sick Century Brewery Co.	Seattle	WA	1825	1944-56
Sicks Brewing Co.	Salem	OR	1301-1302	1944-53
Sicks Great Falls Brewery	Great Falls	MT	603-604	1945-49
Sicks Seattle Brewing & Malt Co.	Seattle	WA	1817-1818	1944-56
Siebens Brewery Co.	Chicago	IL	275-276	1933-67
Silver Foam Brewing Co.	Jackson	MI	530	1934-40
Silver Springs Brewing Co.	Port Orchard	WA	1798	1934-50
Silver Springs Brewing Co.	Tacoma	WA	1810	1934-50
Simon, Wm. Brewery Co.	Buffalo	NY	1068-1072	1933-73
Smith Bros.	New Bedford	MA	389, 469	1937-43
Soo Brewing Co.	Sault Ste Marie	MI	532-533	1939-44
South Bend Brewing Co.	South Bend	IN	331	1936-50
South Bethlehem Brewing Co.	Bethlehem	PA	1696-1698	1933-55
South Fork Brewing Co.	South Fork	PA	1652-1653	1933-40
South Side Brewing Co.	Chicago	IL	90-92, 156, 237	1934-49
Southern Breweries	Norfolk	VA	1792	1935-42
Spoetzl Brewery Co.	Shiner	TX	1788	1933-42
Spokane Brewery Co.	Spokane	WA	1799-1802	1933-44
Sprattler & Mennel Brewing Co.	Paterson	NJ	723	1939-40
Sprenger Brewing Co.	Lancaster	PA	1538, 1622-1623, 1655	1936-51
Springfield Brewing Co.	Springfield	IL	266-267, 270, 278, 282, 456	1933-65
St. Mary's Beverage Co.	St. Marys	PA	1656	1933-40
Stag Brewing Co.	Monongahela	PA	1657	1933-37
Standard Brewing Co.	Cleveland	OH	1192, 1271-1272	1933-61
Standard Brewing Co.	Scranton	PA	1354, 1658-1661, 1708-1709	1934-52
Standard-Rochester Brewing Co.	Rochester	NY	967, 1076-1080, 1092	1933-56
Stanton Brewery Inc.	Troy	NY	978, 1081-1085	1933-51
Star Beverage Co.	Minster	OH	1294	1939-53
Star Brewing Co.	Minster	OH	1273	1933-39
Star Brewing Co.	Vancouver	WA	1826	1935-39
Star Brewing Co.	Lomira	WI	2012-2013	1933-45
Star Brewing Co.	Boston	MA	454-455, 470-472	1934-52
Star Peerless Brewing Co.	Belleville	IL	233, 286-287	1933-57
Star Union Products Co.	Peru	IL	177-178, 272-274, 283-285, 302-303	1933-65
Stecher Brewing Co.	Murphysboro	IL	250	1933-40
Stegmaier Brewing Co.	Wilkes-Barre	PA	1662-1673	1933-55
Stein, Geo. F. Brewing Co.	Buffalo	NY	768-772, 775-777, 800, 1087-1091	1933-57
Stenson Brewing Co.	Chicago	IL	93	1933-43
Sterling Brewers	Evansville	IN	343-344	1933-72
Stevens Point Beverage Co.	Stevens Point	WI	1995	1933-58
Storck Products Co.	Slinger	WI	2011, 2014-2015	1933-35
Storz Brewing Co.	Omaha	NE	616	1933-68
Straub Brewery Co.	St. Marys	PA	1683-1685	1934-39
Stroh Brewing Co.	Detroit	MI	534-536	1933-98
Stroudsburg Brewing Co.	Stroudsburg	PA	1686	1935-37
Sullivan, J.J., Bottled for	Boston	MA	453	1935-40
Sunbury Brewing Co.	Sunbury	PA	1687	1935-37
Sunrise Brewing Co.	Cleveland	OH	1237, 1275	1933-38
Sunset Brewing Co.	Wallace	ID	79	1937-41
Superior Brewing Co.	Chicago	IL	225, 260, 289	1933-41
Terre Haute Brewing Co.	Terre Haute	IN	321-323	1935-58
The Victor Brewing Co.	Jeannette	PA	1674-1676	1934-43
Tip Top Brewing Co.	Cleveland	OH	1276-1277	1938-42
Tivoli Brewing Co.	Detroit	MI	474-477, 537	1933-47
Tivoli-Union Co.	Denver	CO	45-46	1936-54
Trommer, John F. Brewing Co.	Orange	NY	1108-1118	1933-51
Tube City Brewing Co.	McKeesport	PA	1331, 1716-1717	1933-51
Two Rivers Beverage Co.	Two Rivers	WI	1861-1862, 1911, 2027-2028	1933-46
Union Brewing Co.	New Castle	PA	1641, 1754	1934-47
Union Brewing Co.	Scranton	PA	1720-1722	1933-43
United Brewing Co.	Newark	NJ	733	1933-34
United States Brewing Co.	Chicago	IL	173-174, 200-201, 255-258	1934-55
United Union Breweries Co.	Walla Walla	WA	1827	1936-45
United Union Brewing Co.	Walla Walla	WA	1808-1809	1935-39
Utica Brewing Co.	Utica	NY	852-855	1934-58
Van Buren Products Co.	Buffalo	NY	804-806	1940-47
Vernon Brewing Co.	Vernon	CA	21	1934-43
Vienna Brewing Co.	Cincinnati	OH	1281	1938-49
Wacker Brewing Co.	Lancaster	PA	1520, 1559, 1731	1938-57
Wagner Brewing Co.	Granite City	IL	306	1933-38
Wagner, John Co.	Sidney	OH	1267	1934-38
Walter Brewing Co.	Pueblo	CO	1470-49	1933-60
Walter Brewing Co.	Eau Claire	WI	2018-2022	1933-60
Walter Bros. Brewing Co.	Wenasha	WI	1897-1899, 1907-1909	1934-57
Walter, Geo. Brewing Co.	Appleton	WI	1834	1933-71
Warsaw Brewing Co.	Warsaw	IL	120-122, 228	1935-72

Brewery	City	State	Reference Numbers	In Business
Washington Breweries	Columbus	OH	1225, 1285-1286	1935-52
Washington Brewing Co.	Washington	PA	1572, 1732-1734	1934-40
Wausau Brewing Co.	Wausau	WI	1831-1833, 2008-2009	1934-61
Wayne Brewing Co.	Erie	PA	1735-1736	1933-51
Webb Corporation	East Liverpool	OH	1160, 1288, 1290, 1293	1933-52
Weber Waukesha Brewing Co.	Waukesha	WI	2023-2026	1934-58
Weber, G. Brewing Co.	Theresa	WI	1991-1992	1934-60
Wehle Brewing Co.	West Haven	CT	50-51, 62, 70-71	1933-43
Weisbrod & Hess Brewing Co.	Philadelphia	PA	1737-1738	1933-37
Wentzler Brewery Co.	Lykens	PA	1739	1933-39
West Bend Brewing Co.	West Bend	WI	1973	1936-72
West Bend Lithia Co.	West Bend	WI	1941-1942	1934-54
West End Brewing Co.	Utica	NY	941, 954, 1120-1129	1933-50
West Masontown Brewery Co.	Masontown	PA	1404	1934-39
Western Brewery Co.	St. Louis	MO	601	1936-54
Western Brewery Co.	Belleville	IL	279-280	1936-54
Westminster Brewing Co.	Chicago	IL	153, 232	1933-37
White Eagle Brewing Co.	Chicago	IL	86-87, 132-133, 308-310	1933-50
Whitewater Brewing Co.	Whitewater	WI	1839-1840, 1880	1933-43
Widman Brewing Co.	Bethlehem	PA	1640, 1747	1934-38
Wiedemann, Geo. Brewing Co.	Newport	KY	361, 364	1934-69
Williams, Roger Brewing Corp.	Providence	RI	1783	1935-39
Wisconsin Cooperative Brewery	Grafton	WI	1879	1937-42
Wittekindt, Wm. J. Brewing Co.	Evansville	IN	345	1937-40
Woerner Brewing Co.	Reading	PA	1748	1935-38
Wolf, John Jacob	Philadelphia	PA	1749	1933-36
Worcester Brewing Co.	Worcester	MA	459	1945-62
Wunderbrau Brewing Co.	Cincinnati	OH	1295	1951-56
Yakima Valley Brewing Co.	Selah	WA	1821	1934-54
Yonkers Colonial Corp.	Yonkers	NY	1139-1140	1934-38
Yough Brewing Co.	Connellsville	PA	1755-1756	1934-41
Youngstown Brewing Co.	Youngstown	OH	1221-1222, 1234, 1274	1935-44
Yuengling, D. G. & Sons, Inc.	Pottsville	PA	1757-1761	1934-48
Zeman Brewing Co.	Mundelein	IL	315-317	1942-64
Ziegler, Louis Brewing Co.	Beaver Dam	WI	1919, 2030-2031	1935-49
Zieglers Old Fashioned Brewing Co.	La Crosse	WI	1960	1946-48
Zoller Brewing Co.	Davenport	IA	350	1933-44
Zynda Brewing Co.	Detroit	MI	484	1933-38

Country	Reference Numbers	In Business
England?	2034	L40s-E50s
Germany	2035, 2037, 2040-2046, 2053-2055, 2059, 2061-2066	L40s-E50s
Canada	2036, 2050-2052, 2056-2057	L40s-E50s
Mexico	2038-2039	L40s-E50s
Holland	2047-2049	L40s-E50s
Poland	2058	L40s-E50s
Czechoslovakia	2060	L40s-E50s

Index of States